PRAISE FOR *PARENTING RIGHT FROM THE START*

"Authentic, practical, and important, *Parenting Right From the Start* guides parents to explore how our patterns can hinder or support our path to becoming the parents we want to be. Dr. Vanessa's message that our ongoing development is intricately linked to who our children become paves the way for parenting that is connected, rewarding, and meaningful."

TINA PAYNE BRYSON, PHD bestselling coauthor of *The Whole-Brain Child* and *No-Drama Discipline*

"This is the book the world has been waiting for. It is the absolute best exploration of early parenting, gifting parents with so many beautiful understandings of this ancient and sacred dance. Dr. Vanessa effortlessly merges the latest in the science of growing babies into children with the simultaneous growing of parents into conscious, capable, caring grown-ups with lots of passion and swagger!"

MAGGIE DENT author of the bestselling *Mothering Our Boys* and other books

"A wise and encouraging guide to nurturing the life-changing connection between you and your child. This isn't a book that serves up pat formulas or that relies on one-size-fits-none parenting strategies. It's about leaning into your own hard-earned parenting wisdom: your growing knowledge of what it's going to take to nurture and raise this one-of-a-kind child."

ANN DOUGLAS bestselling author of *Happy Parents, Happy Kids* and CBC Radio parenting columnist

"Dr. Vanessa shows us that parents can choose the kind of parent they want to be. Grounded in the science of child development, *Parenting Right From the Start* is empowering, inspirational, and practical! A must read for new parents and caregivers."

MARILYN PRICE-MITCHELL, PHD developmental psychologist and author of *Tomorrow's Change Makers*

"A brilliant, soulful, and insightful book on the primacy of early years. A vivid expression of the Conscious Parenting principle of Child Honouring, this work touts the importance of parents' self-awareness in raising their young. Connection and compassion shine in Dr. Vanessa's parenting wisdom."

RAFFI CAVOUKIAN CM, OBC, singer, author, Raffi Foundation for Child Honouring

"Kids can be complicated and confusing. Dr. Vanessa's book is the one every parent needs to be able to navigate the white waters of parenting with a level of grace and ease. If every parent read this book we could change the world within the next generation for the greater good of humanity."

KERWIN RAE creator of the podcast *Unstoppable*, entrepreneur, and international speaker

"Parents have come to know and trust Dr. Vanessa's smart and relatable advice. *Parenting Right From the Start* is a warm, evidence-based guide that invites us to examine the complicated stuff we bring to the parenting experience. It is going straight to the top of my list of books to give new parents."

BRANDIE WEIKLE *Toronto Star* parenting columnist and host of *The New Family* podcast

"I appreciated the brilliant way in which Dr. Vanessa amalgamates developmental science with maternal wisdom to address the most pertinent issues we must consider as parents without pangs of guilt or pressure. This book encapsulates the science and soul of parenting, and is delivered from the heart."

DR. KRISTY GOODWIN author of *Raising Your Child in a Digital World*

"Insightful, engaging, and wise, *Parenting Right From the Start* provides the gentle encouragement parents need to build their child's emotional health while showing parents the way to 'grow you so you can grow them.'"

MONA DELAHOOKE, PHD author of *Beyond Behaviors: Using Brain Science and Compassion to Understand and Solve Children's Behavioral Challenges*

"Overwhelmed and frustrated parents, rejoice! Dr. Vanessa's new book is a much-needed guide to finding peace and wisdom while riding the roller coaster of parenthood. Dr. Vanessa shows the way from worry to confidence."

TOM HOBSON author of *Teacher Tom's First Book* and Teacher Tom's blog

"Parents often ask 'what do we do when this happens' when we should ask, 'how do we *be* when this happens?' Dr. Vanessa has written a wonderful, accessible book about how to *be* what our children need. What she writes and how she lives should inspire us all."

DAVID LOYST MSc (SLP), autism consultant, parent educator

"Soon-to-be parents and parents of young children, listen to Dr. Vanessa's wisdom. The space between the parents is the playground of the child. Her book invites you on a journey to grow yourself as a person so that your child can bathe in the energy of your contented parenting."

HEDY SCHLEIFER founder of Encounter-Centered Transformation and director for the Tikkun Learning Center

"*Parenting Right From the Start* is the book I have been waiting for to recommend to all my clients: those who have children or are planning to have children and those who have ever been a child. Dr. Vanessa's message to parents to do their own work and grow themselves up so that they can be in that exquisite place of *in charge with compassion* may be the most important message of all."

GILA GOLUB counsellor, The Work of Gila Golub

"To give your babies the best start, you need to read this book right from the start. It will give you a greater understanding of how a child's development unfolds but also of the impact of your own early experiences on your parenting journey."

CORA BOECKER early intervention specialist with the Infant Development Program

"*Parenting Right From the Start* is a gift for all parents and their children. With warmth, wisdom, and strong scientific grounding, Dr. Vanessa brings us back to our parenting hearts. This book is a soulful, intelligent, and practical resource so we can parent with richness and realness."

KAREN YOUNG author, child and adolescent specialist, founder of HeySigmund.com

"Dr. Vanessa writes to us from her heart and from a vast store of experience and knowledge. Many of us will read this important book and dearly wish we knew what it contained back when our children were young. But *Parenting Right From the Start* is a book for all of us now no matter where we are as parents or grandparents."

DR. DANA BRYNELSEN OBC, LLD (Hon), former provincial advisor, Infant Development Program of BC

PARENTING RIGHT
FROM
THE START

PARENTING RIGHT
FROM
THE START

LAYING A HEALTHY FOUNDATION
IN THE BABY AND TODDLER YEARS

DR. VANESSA LAPOINTE
Author of *Discipline Without Damage*

RIVER GROVE
BOOKS

Published by River Grove Books
Austin, TX
www.rivergrovebooks.com

Distributed by River Grove Books

Design and composition by Setareh Ashrafologhalai
Cover design by Setareh Ashrafologhalai
Author photo: Lindsay Faber Photography

Publisher's Cataloging-in-Publication data is available.

Print ISBN: 978-1-966629-85-6

eBook ISBN: 978-1-928055-39-6

First Edition

CONTENTS

For Nathan and Maxwell
With my eternal love for all that you
are and all that you inspire.

For David
Thank you for showing up for you,
and then for us—I love you infinity.

For Gila
You truly are doing the most important work
of all—you showed me what love really is.

FOREWORD

W E ALL KNOW that parenting is *the* hardest task in the entire world. Nothing challenges us more than raising these little humans. In my own foray on this journey, I was constantly befuddled by all the advice I was getting and felt overwhelmed trying to decide what kind of parent I wanted to be: Tiger? Helicopter? Lawnmower? Who was I? What was my parenting style? Frankly, I spent the early years of my parenting searching for the answers to these questions and finding none. I felt as many parents feel—desperate and frustrated.

It was then I realized I had been looking in the wrong places. The answers couldn't come from the traditional models of parenting as they espoused control before connection. I was seeking the opposite: connection before control. The answers needed to emerge from within my own consciousness and through the elevation of my own inner awareness and worth.

It was here that the seeds of conscious parenting were birthed. It was here, through my own struggles as a mother, desperate to connect better with my daughter, that I discovered a passion for conscious parenting and began to write books on it. I truly believe conscious parenting is the only way we will evolve as a planet and heal the next generations of children. This is why I am supportive of this wonderful book by Dr. Vanessa Lapointe; it encapsulates the message of conscious parenting in an artful and insightful manner. Those who read *Parenting Right From the Start* will delight in its eloquence and grace.

Dr. Vanessa's book intuitively captures the power that parenting has to transform the inner world of the parent and thereby, the child. Firmly grounded in the principles of conscious parenting, this book speaks to the challenges *every* parent faces—from sleep struggles to toileting troubles to sibling rivalry. In this unique work, Dr. Vanessa has merged consciousness with the beautiful principles of attachment to help parents practice concrete skills with their children in real time.

Dr. Vanessa's own personal experiences as a mother, combined with her decades of professional expertise, allows her to write with passion, relevance, and remarkable compassion for the unique journeys each one of us undergoes in the parenting process. You will read her words and immediately feel a significant shift in connection with your children. You will understand what has been blocking you and you will discover the courage it takes to remove these barriers to what you desire most: a close relationship with your most beloved children.

When I met Dr. Vanessa at one of my workshops, I knew immediately that here was a woman who not only was a heartfelt mother, but also a highly talented psychologist. She has the capacity to understand the human spirit like few can, and she's able to communicate her insights with an ease that is truly transformational. It makes me so proud to be part of this book's journey into the world because I know it has tremendous power to change how parents treat their children. Read it, absorb it, and find a wonderful path of truer connection with your children.

SHEFALI TSABARY, PHD
Author of *The Awakened Family* and *The Conscious Parent*

INTRODUCTION
START AS YOU WISH TO GO

WILL NEVER FORGET how it felt to find out that I was expecting my first son. I was a graduate student at the time, and had eyes only for the finish line of convocation. Four years and I would have a doctoral degree. Finally, I would be able to practise in my chosen field. But the universe had other plans. Around the end of my first year of doctoral studies I began to wonder if I had a low-grade virus or some other illness that was causing me to be so fatigued all the time. I booked an appointment with my physician, determined to get to the bottom of it. Imagine my surprise when test results revealed that I was pregnant. The father of my children had the wisdom to snap a picture of me right in that moment. The look on my face says it all: absolute disbelief mixed with a significant glimmer of excitement. I didn't know it yet, but right then and there everything changed.

Not long after, I had a miscarriage scare. As I was rushed in for an ultrasound, I remember thinking, "I have only known the possibility of this baby for two short weeks. How am I so attached to him already?" At that point, I had been pregnant for only about ten weeks, but when the flickering image of my son's little heart finally presented itself on that ultrasound screen I sobbed with relief. In fact, I cried so intensely and for so long that the technician insisted I pull it together so she could complete her exam.

From there, I found it difficult to relax into the certainty of the pregnancy. I made many worried visits to my physician, thinking something must be wrong. At one such appointment I said to her, "I just can't wait for him to be born. Then I can stop worrying!" She looked at me with the knowing eyes of a mother and a professional who has seen it all. "Oh, sweetheart," she said, "that's when the real worrying begins." I didn't want to believe her—and in truth, there's been so much good alongside the rest that the scales have certainly balanced—but, in a way, she was right.

I was not prepared emotionally or otherwise for parenthood, despite being a psychologist in the making. I watched my baby son closely. I revelled in the miracle of him while fretting about his current cold. I delighted in his first smiles, in those moments when his sweet toes made their way to his mouth, and even when I was surprised by a baby boy's wayward plumbing. But alongside all of that, I felt a shift in me that was unsettling. I knew something about who I was, and I understood myself as changed, but I couldn't quite put my finger on how.

As happens, I had so many things to consider as a parent. Should I sleep train or not? Should I baby-wear? Is child-led weaning and feeding the way to go? Is my baby supposed to be socializing with other babies? Is co-sleeping okay or not? How do I manage behaviour when those first tantrums emerge? Like many parents, I turned to medical practitioners for advice, as well as to other parents, my own parents, my in-laws, and my siblings who were raising children. The messages were mixed, and they left me feeling more confused.

I remember thinking I had no choice but to sleep train. I sat outside my baby's door, trying to take to heart his father's reassurance that we were doing the right thing. I lasted four awful minutes. As a graduate student, my clinical supervisor had trained me on what constituted a "good timeout." I tried it. Once. It also felt awful. I joined a baby and parent group for the socialization because that's what new moms did, but I felt like my baby needed time with me most of all. I determined I would stop breastfeeding when it felt naturally right, despite some social pressure to "cut the apron strings."

After each of these uncertain moments, that unsettled part of me would rear up and ask: What if I'm doing it wrong? What if I've failed? What if I'm not good enough? What if I've messed it all up? There was a constant battle between the ill-boding script running in my mind and my deeply felt sense that I *could* do this—that I was good enough, that there was no possible way I could mess this up as long as I listened to myself. My *real* self. Not my assumed self. My *wise* self. Not my fearful self. My *intuitive* self. Not my reactive self. I was self-assured enough to determine my own way about sleep training and co-sleeping, about compassionate discipline, and myriad other decisions. Sometimes I hit the mark and other times I didn't.

As I walked on in my journey of parenthood and witnessed my children walking their journey of development, it would be some time before I understood what was happening inside of me for my own growth and, simultaneously, outside of me for the growth of each of my children. There were many fretful years of parenting a child with developmental and learning differences, a child with behavioural challenges, and a child with some medical hiccups; many years of figuring out who I was as a person and as a parent; and many years of struggling within a marriage in the context of this change. And then something happened.

I woke up.

You see, it was as though I was asleep, playing out my life in a dazed, dreamlike state. A true grasp of what was happening was ever so slightly beyond my reach. Unbeknownst to my rational and intellectual self, I was beginning to converge on a life-altering idea: that before I would be able to help my babies grow up to be the kind human beings I dreamed they would be, I first had to grow myself up. This meant realizing that my perspective, and all the feelings that flowed from that, was inspired by my internal self. That internal self was a culmination of my life's experiences, especially those from childhood, when my impressionable mind was being formed. And so, in order to grow myself up, I had to understand my childhood experiences anew. This was the only way I'd be able to make sense of why I grew up to see the world as I do.

I didn't have the luxury of doing my inner work on a therapist's couch—I had to do it on my feet in the full colour of life. I had to accept that any angst I felt as a parent had nothing to do with my children, their apparent challenges, or the ups and downs of parenting. Rather, that angst came from the un-grown parts of myself. The two-year-old me who learned to be frightened when scary things happened. The four-year-old me who learned to be ashamed when scolded for my behaviour. The six-year-old me who learned to be unsettled when I worried my parents would divorce. And it isn't like I had a terrible childhood. This is just my story, and these are my feelings. You will have your own. We all do. But when I started to make sense of where my feelings came from, I also started to make sense of why parenthood had unsettled me, why I had all this worry in me, and what needed to shift so I could step in with the energy in which I wanted my children to be bathed.

How did this—and does this continue—to play out in my life as a parent? Only every moment of every day! Some of those moments are big and some are small. For example, when my youngest son developed hearing and language exceptionalities, I had to connect with my fear of the future for him, my distress at how his school years would almost certainly play out, and my drive to control the factors that I perceived to be contributing to his circumstances.

Once I connected with that fear, distress, and need for control, I realized those feelings came from a long-ago time, a time when my neural connections were wiring up and things around me felt distressing and out of control.

The mind sees only what it believes, and what it believes is based on our experiences. Those beliefs will colour everything that happens in our lives, as parents and otherwise. The best part is that as all-encompassing as beliefs are in their influence over our lives, there is nothing absolute about them. They can change. Our beliefs are misty, nebulous, and fabricated. They are a concocted narrative that emerges out of a collection of occurrences. As William Faulkner brilliantly wrote, "The past is never dead. It is not even the past."[1] We see life only through the lens of our earlier experiences. Dr. Helen Schucman, clinical psychologist and author of *A Course in Miracles*, tells us that "we see only the past."[2] We aren't seeing reality or absolute truth. We are seeing our version of it. When unaware of this, we are essentially blinded by our beliefs. We cannot see what is happening, and that means "we are never upset for the reasons we think."[3] We are upset because we are peering through a veil of childhood wounds. We fall into those wounds when a present-day circumstance sends us back in time and triggers the feelings we would have had as young children when—even with the best, well-intentioned parents—our needs were not fully met. When we are in a wound, we are by definition age-regressed. We are responding from our three-year-old or four-year-old self. My belief as a child that things were uncertain created the experience of fear and distress, and the feeling of being overwhelmed. So, when challenges arose in my adult life (as a parent or otherwise), I could only react through the lens of fear, distress, and overwhelm, seeking control.

My son's situation provided a gift. It triggered those feelings, which gave me a chance to look at them and to grow myself up in light of the new understanding that was emerging from my self-growth process. I understood that it was my little-girl self who was scared, distressed, and even frantic for control, not my mama self. And with this realization, the little-girl pieces of me could rest in the assurance that all was well, that my grown-up self could be trusted to take the lead and find the way through.

With this more settled existence, my ability to be present for my son completely shifted. I could see the gift in the challenge and the veil that had been lifted to reveal a path of hope, support, intervention, and growth. Only through these experiences of growing myself have I become more available to my role as a parent. I know now that my boys' earliest years, as well as their present growth and development, would have been different had I understood what was happening within me prior to their arrival. I would have parented right from the start with less angst and more swagger. If I'd known—through all the normal, beautiful, loud, chaotic, fun moments of my sons' early years—that I was responding to them from my child self during periods of angst or uncertainty, they would have benefited from bathing in the warm energy of my contentment instead of the stifling energy of my alarm. It's possible that this would have smoothed out parts of their path. But it didn't turn out that way, and as a result, they have had the gift of figuring things out as have I—and that in itself is perfection.

MY JOB AS a psychologist is to help children grow in the best possible way. I always feel humbled and privileged to walk alongside parents in their journey of raising their children and helping them to grow up. Many of my clients are parents with children over the age of three who are presenting with challenges such as mental health issues, developmental exceptionalities, suicidal tendencies, self-harm, rebellion, or other difficulties along their developmental journey. During my almost twenty years of working to support parents and children through all sorts of challenges—and in figuring it out personally along the way—I have come to an understanding. I believe that many of these issues could potentially have been prevented if things had happened differently in the child's first few years of life. These first precious years are crucial when it comes to laying the foundation for what follows.

And yet, the dominant pop culture often has parents raising their babies, toddlers, and preschoolers in ways that are no longer supported by the science of child development. We fall into this pop-culture parenting trap because of the transfer of beliefs, from one generation to the next, about who children really are. The "original sin" view of the child, for example, prevalent in the Middle Ages and into the early 1600s, propagated the sense that children are born full of evil and require adult direction to be purged of it. In the late 1600s, the "blank slate" view had adults believing that children were hollow vessels just waiting to be filled and moulded by our guiding hand. And let's not forget the "flowery meadows" view, popular in the 1700s, which had grown-ups somewhat neglectfully releasing their children to the proverbial flowery meadows to blossom without adult interference. Though none among us would likely admit to a staunch espousing of any of these biases, the reality is that their influence continues to invade the minutiae of day-to-day parenting. We are irritated by the inconvenience of *development* and want to hurry it up with techniques and strategies. We are frustrated when children don't respond as we think they should. We set consequences and mete out punishments to get them to fall into line. Well-intentioned, all of it, but also antiquated and out of touch with the science—and heart—of child development.

Beyond the invasion of bias, our dominant child-raising pop culture has also flourished due to the misguided twisting of developmental science to suit the needs of the time-starved, outcome-focused modern world. We don't have time for development to play out naturally, so we try to hurry it along. We seek experts who can crack the code and give us tricks and strategies to this end. We fret about university acceptance and life success almost from a child's first breath. We hyper-schedule our children's lives with enrolment in every possible enriching extracurricular activity to make sure they are in the running, forgetting that nature already has a brilliant plan in the works that will have our child in the lead by a long shot.

But how are soon-to-be parents and parents of young children to know all of this? There is no parenting handbook that walks you through the importance of doing a deep dive into your familial history to understand your biases, to grasp the influences that shaped your own mind, and to come to terms with how all of this might affect what you bring to the raising of your own child. That non-existent handbook also fails to explain the advances that have been made in the psychology and understanding of child-raising practices. It can literally take the accumulated experience of a few graduate degrees in psychology and child development, sloshing your way through the trenches with a child or two, and spending your life's fortune on psychotherapy to make sense of it. And who does that as part of the preparation for baby's arrival? "Honey, I think we should go with a neutral colour in the nursery—and also, let's review our family tree to see what fear-based parenting practices might have been transmitted down the line," said probably no soon-to-be parent ever. Is it any wonder, then, that there are very few (if any) among us who can honestly say that we were completely ready for the tidal wave of emotion and the life-changing interpersonal dynamics that can unravel even the most robust new parent?

During the emotional roller coaster and challenges of welcoming a child to the world, many parents are overwhelmed and frustrated. Since children don't arrive clutching a manual, parents sometimes tend to raise them according to the practices of past generations. But it doesn't have to be that way. Today, we can draw on the very latest science of child development, and an ever-deepening understanding of the complex psychological interplay between parental self-growth and a child's healthy growth. Combined, these gifts offer parents an opportunity to raise their children well, right from the start.

This is what brings me—and, I hope, you—to this book. It is my greatest hope that I might offer all parents an alternative path, one that is fuelled by the science of child development, the very best that psychology offers, and my own journey as a mother. I believe this is a better path than those we have been treading thus far. A path that will allow you to raise a human being, from the beginning, in exactly the way nature intended. A path that will allow you to start as you wish to go, and an overview of where to begin your journey so it feels tangible and approachable rather than ethereal and slightly beyond reason. A path that may keep you out of my office with your behaviourally challenging six-year-old, your anxious and overwhelmed nine-year-old, your reactive and tuned-out fourteen-year-old, or your despairing and undone eighteen-year-old. A path that will have you laying a conscious and informed foundation for your child's upbringing before they take their first breath, or at least early on enough in their sweet little life that the foundation you've laid will require only slight tweaks and modifications (and not full demolition!) in order to be truly spectacular. A path that will not only have your child growing as nature intended but will also leave you open to receiving the greatest gift you will ever be offered. I'm talking about the gift of growing up yourself—a gift that will allow you to live your fullest, best life and, along the way, be fully available to your child as they do their own growing. And the best thing about this gift? It comes direct from your child's heart.

This book is organized into two parts. Part one provides a clear, easy-to-understand foundation that will set you up for really making sense of how to support your growing little. I pull back the curtain on the human mind so that you can understand the origins of your own big feelings about parenthood. I explain the science of attachment and walk you through exactly how this essential-to-life relationship forms between you and your baby. I take you into the inner workings of the growing brain so you can see what is happening for your child as you literally direct their neurons to connect in specific ways. I will reveal to you the natural hierarchy of the parent-child relationship and champion you to head out of the gates fully in the lead, so your child can rest capably into your care. And I will share with you the secret wonder of why toddler tantrums are a parenting win, and how healthy development includes lots of ups and downs. At the end of part one, you'll find "Dr. Vanessa's Parenting Principles"—a handy primer to remind you of what you most need to absorb from this book in order to parent right from the start.

In part two, we get down to the work of applying all that is explained in part one to the nitty-gritty reality of your everyday parenting life. Are you trying to sort out the always-tricky issue of sleep? Do you have a child who is refusing to feed, or nursing constantly, or has become incredibly picky about food? Do you have a little one who is biting or hitting or kicking? I'll help you navigate the wild world of toilet training, figure out what sibling rivalry is really all about, and manage the transition that occurs when new adults, such as caregivers, are introduced to your child's life.

It's typically said that babies don't come with a manual, but perhaps this book is that manual. Read on. You've got this. You really can parent right from the start. And if at any point you feel unsure about that, just know that I've got you. We'll get there together, one chapter at a time.

PART
ONE

A PARENT IS BORN

Y THE TIME I finished graduate school I had spent more than half my life dreaming of becoming a psychologist. Finally, after thirteen years of post-secondary study, gruelling written and oral exams, and the completion of three degrees, I landed my first job. I was ecstatic! As my start date approached, I focused on being prepared. I knew I had the book smarts to do this work, but I wanted to show up for that first job like nobody had ever shown up for a job before. I assembled what I thought to be a perfect "capable psychologist" wardrobe. I wrote out lists of questions that parents might ask so I could rehearse potential answers. I reviewed diagnostic texts, ensuring I had the information firmly encoded in my memory. I was ready. And then, three days before the job was to start, I was leaning over my little son when he jumped up unexpectedly. His very solid head hit mine, breaking my nose. I ended up greeting my very first clients with two black eyes and a swollen face. All the preparation in the world, and then—SLAM.

As it turns out, parenting is a bit like this. Most of us prepare for parenting, which is understandable since it's arguably the most important job we'll ever have and we want to get it right. We paint the baby's room, buy a stroller and a crib, and practise changing diapers on other people's babies. As our own baby's appearance day draws near, we feel more or less ready for showtime.

Then your child arrives. You feel the earth move underneath you. Your axis tilts. You are in the midst of one of the most incredible psychological and emotional shifts a human being can experience: you are now a parent, responsible for another life in this world. Suddenly, there is a new North Star guiding your big choices and your smaller everyday decisions. And you are keenly aware that those choices and decisions will shape your child, a thought that is both exciting and scary. You thought you were prepared, and then—SLAM.

The hard-to-grasp truth is that parenting right from the start begins much earlier than the weeks and months before your baby is born. In fact, it begins long before you even decide to have a child. The act of parenting is shaped by how you see, interpret, and respond to the world around you. And this world view took shape in your mind long before you became an adult, let alone a parent.

Some people shift into parenthood with more ease than others, though most admit to struggles along the way. Despite all our careful prepping and planning, many of us find it hard to get our bearings. We may worry that we'll never master this round-the-clock parenting gig, given that the job description changes almost daily. Just as we get the hang of the three-naps-a-day schedule, it's suddenly time to deal with two naps and more frequent night wakings. Or maybe we've made it through the first wave of separation anxiety only to be confronted with the onset of toddler tantrums. Every time we think we're in a groove, our child's development changes, and we must keep grooving right along with them.

Through it all, our minds may be partially off-line. Not simply because of fatigue, but also because we may not understand the subconscious forces that are driving us. And yet, these forces—a series of beliefs buried so deep within our psyche that we may not even know they exist—colour all we perceive and do as parents.

You'll certainly be aware of some of these beliefs, such as your views on education or household rules. But many more operate on a subconscious level. You may believe that you're not good enough, for instance, or that you must always please others ahead of yourself, or that you are not worthy of receiving love and affection. You may believe that as a parent you should be all-powerful, or that your child should be happy just because you want them to be. Whatever your beliefs—and regardless of whether they are conscious or unconscious—you will feel their effect, especially in those yucky moments that all parents experience from time to time, when you're overwhelmed and full of self-doubt and guilt.

Soon enough, you'll discover an interesting thing about parenting: you will do things for your children that you might not do for yourself. I was a competitive figure skater until the age of sixteen. My mother spent many hours driving me to and from practices and competitions, sitting rinkside watching me, and sewing and adorning costumes. Now in her early seventies, she will tell you that she never spent a fraction of that time doing what she should have done for herself—activities such as exercising, seeing her friends, and making time for her own hobbies. Why would she forego her life for mine? Because she believed, as many parents do, that self-sacrifice is what it means to be a "good" parent. We say and do all sorts of things as parents, some of which we love, some of which we hate, and much of which we are barely aware of and would struggle to explain.

You may find that being a parent can also stir up challenging emotions and experiences. For example, what if you were the kind of organized, methodical, and logical person who always kept a tidy home and prided yourself on your same-day email turnaround? Then one morning you realize you haven't showered in three days, you are still carrying your baby weight, your house is caked in dirt, the sink is full of unwashed dishes, you have mountains of laundry to do, and growing piles of paperwork are demanding your attention. "What happened to me?" you think. "I'm a mess!" *Bam!* You are seven years old again, feeling inadequate compared to your older, more capable sibling, and worried that the world is laughing at your incompetence.

What if I told you that in the midst of the laundry, the dirty dishes, and the self-doubt, you would be hit squarely on the nose by the opportunity of a lifetime? That part of doing right by your child includes seizing the significant opportunity that parenting provides for your *own* growth? Would you take that on at full throttle knowing that it would serve not only you but also your child? This is the powerful gift that comes with being a parent. Parenting is a transformative wake-up call that beckons us to fully emerge into the human beings we were meant to become.

You know that feeling you get when you're sleeping peacefully and then your alarm sounds and shocks you into alertness? Well, when you're blissfully unaware of the growing up that you may still need to do, becoming a parent is exactly like that—jarring and unpleasant. But don't let that deter you. Time to wake up, sleepyhead! Your full and beautiful life as a parent is waiting for you.

The experiences shared by the many parents I have worked with in my clinical practice over almost twenty years, as well as my own experiences as a mom, have shown me that parenthood is full of joyful moments. There's the wonder of watching your child grow right in front of you—first smiles, first steps, first words. The feeling of warmth that fills you when a smile breaks out on her sweet little face as you walk through the door. The squishy tenderness of his pudgy little hand reaching absent-mindedly for yours. It isn't all work.

But you will definitely have moments—maybe many of them— that will smack you in the face. I'm not talking here about feeling angst-ridden over the colour of your baby's poop, or sleep schedule, or an older sibling's acceptance, or whether it's time for solid food.

That would be too easy. What I'm talking about are the moments of doubt or unease that settle over you, a feeling that you just can't put your finger on, regardless of whether you are a new or experienced parent. It might be the pervasive sense that something is wrong, or a niggling feeling of depression that won't lift. It might be the awareness that you are constantly in conflict with others (your partner, family, or friends) over parenting issues. Maybe you find yourself acting in ways that you don't want to act. And maybe you come to the uncomfortable realization that "I am turning into my mother/father," or "I don't want to be a yelly-shouty parent, so why do I behave like this," or "I swore I would have it together and now I feel as if I am falling apart."

The good news is that you don't have to wait for these feelings of doubt and unease to blindside you before addressing and alleviating them. Every person who becomes a parent will experience some version of a wake-up call. It's universal—which means you can expect it and prepare for it. This knowledge is your power. It is the invitation to step into a fuller understanding of what you and your child need in order to grow in the best way. This invitation is exactly why I have written this book. When you understand the powerful impact of the parent-child relationship on growth and development, and your own needs for rest and awareness, you will be more attuned to how to care for yourself and your child. And this, in turn, allows you to avoid being swallowed whole by parenthood's rude awakening, saving you from years of angst and upset.

Over time I've come to understand the two most powerful influences that affect how we parent: one is how we were parented, and the other is our family's history. Research shows that we are likely to replicate the programs of our own parents;[1] that is, we parent as we were parented, even if we swear we won't. Research also shows that the experiences of our ancestral family members are passed along to us through our DNA.[2] Although we may not have experienced what our parents, aunts, uncles, grandparents, and other ancestors have, their feelings and experiences are nevertheless lodged in our genes, and they can manifest in how we respond to our lives as parents and beyond.

The combined effect of these two influences is what I refer to as your "program." Whether consciously or not, you are run by this program. It lives buried within your sense of self and colours everything you see and do. But when you bring that program out of its deep nesting place and into your conscious awareness, you are empowered to do two things: first, you can predict your program's influence on your life and the life of your child; and second, you can rewrite the parts of your program that do not serve healthy growth. This is what I refer to throughout the book as "doing your work."

It is work to acknowledge our deeply entrenched programming. It is work to accept that our interior programs (rather than our unruly and needy children) are what trigger and unsettle us. And it is work to understand ourselves in a new light so that we can live life in the present rather than driven by events that are in our past or buried in our family history.

Keep in mind that even the best parents are simply unable to give growing children everything they may need. This is a static reality of our human existence. However, whether you are already the parent of a baby or young child, are on the cusp of becoming a parent, or are just thinking about bringing a child into your life, this is the time to make deep and conscious decisions about the kind of parent you want to be. In fact, those decisions are the most important step in the growth process for both you and your child.

This is not the time to be daunted and defeated. Even in the most difficult moments, the opportunity exists for parenting to be empowering and inspirational.[3] The shame you feel when enduring the judgmental stares of others during your toddler's meltdown can be transformed into an unwavering understanding of your swagger and competence. Your despair in being overwhelmed by sleepless nights and endless fatigue can be the call you need to understand the limitlessness of your own power. Day in and day out, little and big moments like these offer you the opportunity to choose a story that works for you rather than against you—guaranteed. By exploring these two influences more deeply here, you will be able to understand when they are at work within you, and how best to rewrite your own narrative. And then, duly armed, your choice is in whether or not you answer the call and step into the fullest possible version of spectacular you.

Your Parents' Programs

As you become a parent, one of the most important things you can do is to deeply consider the parent-child relationship you existed within during your formative years. What pieces of that relationship may still need to be understood and transformed within you? Understanding those core psychological and emotional pieces may afford you the opportunity to "grow up" more fully and, in turn, to be available to the growing up of your child.

When you were born you were thrust into the most intimate space of the parent-child relationship. This first experience of relationship is so potent and formative that it serves as the template for all other relationships to come. The way our parents interact with us shapes our brains and ultimately our sense of who we are in this world. This first relationship can dictate much of what we may become in life.

The parent-child relationship can be viewed as a continuum. At one end is the child who experiences being cared for, physically and emotionally, in a consistent manner. Note that I didn't say "in a perfect manner." No parent can ever be perfect. But this template would allow that child to emerge into a solid sense of self, capable of recreating intimacy in other relationships. Statistically, it would also mean that they are much more likely to perform well at school, be healthier, and be less likely to suffer mental health issues.[4]

On the other end of the continuum is the parent-child relationship fraught with challenge. This child's needs were not consistently met. Perhaps it was a relationship in which a parent's long absences or lack of emotional availability resulted in the child feeling abandoned, or one in which a child was maltreated or neglected. This baby is likely to grow into a person who struggles in varying degrees with physical and mental health, relationships, and/or employment.[5]

What you need to know is this: it's virtually impossible for any parent, anywhere, to come into their parenting gig with a neutral, blank slate. Add external societal influences to the mix and it's easy to see how parenting can become a quagmire of unease and self-doubt. And given that we know how formative and all-important the parent-child relationship is, it doesn't take a leap of faith to understand that the prevailing cultural and psychological norms of any parent's day will have a deep influence on that relationship. Resistance is almost futile. So, no pressure!

Your Family History

Though the first source of parental programming is inadvertently passed on by our parents, a second major source comes from generations past via our genes. The collective history of our ancestors is transmitted down the family line through our DNA. The science of epigenetics has revealed that it isn't purely your DNA sequence that determines the expression of those genes. Rather, the conditions around you can turn on or heighten the expression of some genes while turning off or suppressing the expression of others. In this way, experiences—including traumatic ones—are encoded in the body at the cellular level.

The influence of traumatic experiences can be genetically traced through several generations. Psychologist and author Mark Wolynn describes this transmission of trauma powerfully through stories of his clients with family members who died in or lived through the Holocaust, as well as clients who have grandparents, aunts, uncles, or even more distant relatives who experienced the death of a child or witnessed terrible violence or any other perceived trauma. He provides a thorough and accessible scientific account of how this occurs in his book *It Didn't Start with You.*[6]

Take a moment to consider this: females are born with all the eggs they will reproduce from and more. That means that a female's genetic material was inside of her grandmother at the time of her mother's conception, and so on down the line. Given the process of epigenetics, this means that a woman's cells may carry the experiences of her grandmother at a cellular level. For males (who produce new sperm across their lifetime), the link will be stronger with their biological fathers and what was happening in that father's life at the time of the son's conception. However, men and women can inherit genetically coded trauma from either or both of their parents, and hence from either or both of their paternal and maternal lines.

The case histories around intergenerational trauma are eye-opening and numerous. My great-grandmother was separated from her Indigenous tribe when she married a European settler who had come to Canada in pursuit of a better life. After she married, she lost her connection to her people, her village, her community. She gave life to seven children, but sadly she suffered from numerous mental breakdowns until eventually she ended up in an asylum, where she lived until her death. Her young children were farmed out to relatives and orphanages upon her institutionalization, and they endured their own challenging and traumatic experiences.

Time marched on. I came into the world and proceeded to have a fairly typical childhood. My parents eventually divorced. I went on to marry and have my own children, and then I also divorced. During my divorce, I became consumed with the idea of "losing" my children. I wasn't worried that I would lose my children to the child welfare system—there was never any question of that—but moment by moment, issue by issue, as my boys' father and I navigated the first year or two of separation and divorce, I was paralyzed by a single thought: What if they choose their dad over me?

Why was I thinking this? As a child psychologist, I am supposed to be attuned to these types of misperceptions. But even my years of education and experience were no match for genetics. I felt angst over potentially losing my children because the loss of my family system is encoded in my DNA. No matter what is truly happening in my life, I will feel this loss at some level of my consciousness, and will look for ways that this trauma is "real" in my life's circumstances. Knowing the story of my ancestral roots and being aware of the influence of genetically inherited family trauma, I was able to piece together this understanding relatively early on. It was oddly comforting to be able to make sense of my fears in this way, and freeing to know that in the simple act of making the link, I was resolving the issue. I have worked within my own therapeutic process to deepen this resolution and bring a sense of peace into my life instead of fear.

The inheritance of family trauma through DNA is something anyone can experience. Almost always, it involves the replaying of unprocessed trauma—abuse, deaths, scandals, and/or losses that were never talked about, that may have been forbidden topics of conversation, or were buried deep in the skeleton closet. The entire spectacular reality, as Wolynn so aptly details, is a subconscious program coded in your genes. It isn't anything you have done specifically, although if you are reliving family trauma you will likely feel wholly responsible for it. Sometimes inherited family trauma is discernable because of its peculiar and sudden onset, such as the young man who suddenly started having panic attacks after his twenty-first birthday, the age at which his grandfather was wounded in battle during the Second World War. Other times it will play out and continue to manifest in seemingly mysterious ways, and only when the family's historical puzzle is pieced together will what is truly happening become obvious. Major life changes, milestone birthdays, and other notable happenings can often trigger the replaying of a family trauma story.

Becoming a parent is certainly a major life change—and, not surprisingly, even this happy event can be the gateway to the reliving of family trauma. This may be because much of what people historically experience as traumatic within their families often involves children. It's not that children experience traumatic things more often than adults; rather, it's that when bad things happen to kids it tends to be more traumatic than when bad things happen to adults. Trauma has a more devastating impact on children because their brains are not yet developed enough to safeguard them against the effects. The traumatic experience then becomes the organizing force of the young, developing brain (rather than being processed and buffered by the mature brain of an adult).[7] As a result, childhood trauma can have significant and lasting effects. A parent who carries trauma from their own childhood can be triggered when their own child reaches the same life stage at which the trauma was experienced.

Although trauma can be genetically transmitted from one generation to the next, that does not mean there is no escape. The same cellular process that transmits family trauma contains the potential for healing it. Any individual can retroactively process their family's historical experiences to effect real change in their own lives, and in the lives of the entire family system, so that their children will never suffer the same way. Occasionally, with self-reflection, people can accomplish this on their own. More often, especially with deep programs that are having a large impact on an individual's life, reprocessing and healing will require the support of a trained coach, therapist, or healer.

Let's be real for a moment. I write parenting books and counsel parents and kids, but I needed someone to guide me. I couldn't believe that my unconscious mind was running the show. I was reliving old patterns until my counsellor and teacher pointed them out—and then I couldn't stop seeing them. My counsellor introduced me to modalities I'd never heard of. Some included talk therapy; others worked to bring my subconscious mind in line with my conscious mind. For example: I am a child psychologist and a fierce mama; I know that I am awesome and my kids are lucky to have me. Yet when they went to their father's house for a night, I worried they were going to leave me. I tried to talk myself out of this thought but to no avail. My subconscious mind believed this, and my conscious mind doesn't give the orders. My counsellor directed me to a subconscious "healer" who helped me absorb the statement, "My kids will never leave me" until I felt an internal shift. The worry still comes up, but I am able to tend to it now; the walls are no longer crashing down on me.

I also looked for a village of people who would support my personal development. Thankfully, my counsellor had already created one. Every week, she holds a circle filled with people who are facing the challenges raised by their marriages, their children, other relationships, their finances, and their health. They are challenged by the same things I am, and I heal through witnessing their work. When I am challenged by life and stuck in blame and unable to find the opportunity for growth, I can put up my hand and ask for help. When I am not at the circle, I can call any of these people at any time to make sense of what is going on for me. I have created an entirely new village to help me grow myself up while I grow up my children.

Attachment-Centred Parenting

You now have a deeper understanding of the influences working away on how you parent. You know that you bring baggage into this wonderful and exciting role—some that you've carried in on your own, and some that has been passed down to you from generations past. Either way, this new knowledge has put you in a much stronger position to break free of habits that may not be in your child's best interest, or yours. And there really is no better time to take that leap than right now. Society is in the relatively early days of a sea change in our understanding of human development, a change that is leading to a new understanding of what children need from their parents and how their parents can provide it. Thanks in part to contemporary advances in neuroscience and the science of child development, we now know that secure attachment in the relationship between a loving caregiver and a child is utterly essential to a child's healthy growth.

Attachment theory has brought about a radical shift in the study of child development since it was initially developed by John Bowlby and Mary Ainsworth in the 1940s,[8] and more deeply studied and scientifically understood through the 1970s and 1980s. Psychologists such as Edward Tronick, Bruce Perry, Megan Gunnar, and Daniel Siegel have amassed a large body of evidence-based science irrefutably linking attachment to healthy child development.[9] In fact, attachment may be more essential than food in terms of a young child's hierarchy of needs.[10] What this research tells us is that children need to be seen, heard, and responded to by someone who loves them in order to thrive. Along with the concept of consciousness—understanding the programs that live below the surface in us and run our lives—attachment theory is the philosophy on which this book is based.

The Dominance of Behaviourism

As intuitive as attachment-centred parenting might seem, it is a recent development in our pedagogical practices, coming hot on the heels of a far more pervasive and persuasive approach: behaviourism. The driving force behind behaviourist-influenced parenting was that if you wanted good behaviour in a child, your job as the parent was to manipulate that into being. Indeed, this behavioural manipulation would virtue signal that you were a "good" parent. Today's parents (or anyone whose parents were born after the 1930s) were likely raised according to the tenets of behaviourism, which was the psychological and cultural norm of their own parents' day.

A disturbingly far cry from the science-based principles of attachment theory, behaviourism has its roots in Ivan Pavlov's experiments in classical conditioning, such as the iconic one featuring the ringing bell and the salivating dog. But it was John B. Watson who established and promoted behaviourism as a game-changing psychological theory.[11] Watson was an early-twentieth-century American psychologist whose research focused on applying the science of prediction and behavioural control to child development. He went so far as to warn parents, "When you are tempted to pet your child, remember that mother love is a dangerous instrument."[12]

Watson's work influenced renowned American psychologist B.F. Skinner, whose theories came to dominate child psychology in the mid-twentieth century. Skinner's approach was to keep children famished for their parents' love, affection, and approval. Many twentieth-century parents wouldn't have thought to question this approach, which amounted to withholding love and affection in order to control a child's behaviour. Behaviourism has ruled the day for decades in Western society, likely in part due to the outward appearance of quick results. What parents and even scientists failed to realize, however, was that these so-called results were achieved through a devastating sacrificial play. The parent's relationship with the child was wielded as conditional, and it was in rendering conditional a bond we now understand to be essential that a well-behaved child was produced.

One of the earliest societal steps away from behaviourism and toward attachment-focused parenting came with the publication of *The Common Sense Book of Baby and Child Care* by pediatrician Dr. Benjamin Spock. Published in 1946 amid behaviourist fervour, this wildly popular parenting book espoused a more child-centred approach in which parents were encouraged to let their love for their children flow freely, to embrace flexibility over rigidity, to treat children as human beings, and to trust their own intuition as the only true expert on their child. Mothers flocked to buy his book and devoured its contents with relief, making it the second bestselling book of all time (behind the Bible). But Dr. Spock faced a long campaign of public scrutiny and a backlash that blamed him for encouraging mollycoddling, laziness, and a host of social ills. He may have encouraged a step toward attachment, but Dr. Spock was not successful in overriding the popular notions of behaviourism that were deeply entrenched in Western parenting culture.

Unfortunately, of all the psychological theories that influence the pop culture of child-raising, behaviourism is the most dominant, even to this day. You will continue to run into parents (and non-parents!) who are quick to offer advice that feeds off the finger-wagging admonitions of the behaviourists, such as when they advise you to "train" your children using consequences and other disconnection-based antics. Don't fall for it! (I'll explain why not throughout this book, and have written extensively on this in *Discipline Without Damage*.) The bottom line is that the generation of parents influenced by the allure of behaviourism (and who among us has not secretly wished for well-behaved children at one point or another?) would have been hard-pressed to escape trying out some of its tenets on their children—and that includes you.

Above, you learned that you can understand much of your own programming by identifying what was missing from the parenting that was practised on you. As you seek this understanding, you may need a safe place to vent years of anger and sadness. Many of us have tried to explain away our childhood, shut down our feelings, or numb them out. But what we don't express, we repress, and often it will depress. Once you let it out, you may find it easier to call on compassion and remember that your parents were not bad people or terrible parents; they were simply raising you according to the norms of their day, as well as grappling with their own challenges. The science of child development has added more information to the knowledge bank since then, and this includes understanding the negative impact of behaviourism.

What Behavourism Doesn't Get

The trouble with the behaviourist approach is that it lacks an understanding of three key areas in the development of a child: attachment, developmental awareness, and consciousness. Each is crucial to understanding why a child behaves the way they do. Parenting right from the start includes creating a solid foundation for your child that grows from these three concepts. Let's explore how each of them can infuse your parenting with the most up-to-date principles in child development science.

Attachment

Attachment-centred parenting emphasizes the importance of relationship and connection. As a basic rule of the human condition, our most significant emotional and psychological events, both positive and negative, will occur during our first six years of life. This is because (a) we form our deepest attachments with our most significant caregivers during this formative time, and (b) this is when a child's brain is wiring up at the rate of approximately one million new neural connections per second.[13] You grow as you go.

Dr. Gordon Neufeld, a noted psychologist, has explored in detail how we move through the process of "becoming attached" in the first six years of life.[14] During this process we are danced into our sense of self, into who we are and how we will be in this life. Naturally, there will be other formative influences and experiences in the years to come, but the most influential foundation is laid in those first six years. The takeaway? During those first six years of a child's life, parents have the most powerful opportunity to reach into that growing brain and wire it up in the best possible way.

Since love and human connection are essential to healthy growth and development, the human child is born programmed and wired to seek out this connection constantly. There is no rest and no growth for the human child in the absence of this connection. All of the child's energy goes to ensuring the connection is maintained, which leaves little to direct to the task of growing up. And knowing that children are wired to pursue that connection at all costs, it comes as no surprise to learn that children understandably become eager to restore it, should it be interrupted. Often, though, disconnection is mistakenly co-opted in the name of "discipline." This happens when parents purposely interrupt the connection to alarm the child into seeking reconnection by halting whatever behaviour they are engaged in. Timeouts offer one example of how disconnection can be used to get a child to behave. Others include consequences, the removal of privileges, reward systems, and any other parenting "strategy" that has at its core the spirit of disconnection. Even a tactic like orchestrating a fake "leaving behind" scenario to persuade an uncooperative child to follow plays on a disconnected approach.

If you are in the midst of sourcing parenting "strategies," you've probably uncovered a mountain of disconnection-based approaches (and virtually nothing that would have you leading your child along the trajectory of their optimal growth and development). Any parenting expert who suggests that they have the art of parenting distilled down to a three-step strategy or has attempted to script you through a one-size-fits-all, tightly regimented routine of discipline will rely on disconnection-based approaches, almost without fail, to manipulate the behaviour of children. Child development specifically, and the human condition generally, does not lend itself to regimented, scripted, concocted tricks and strategies. These approaches are mere temptations, luring parents with a purportedly quick fix because they appear easier, tidier, and more convenient than the alternative. But the long view shows us that children need connection. Full stop. They do not need tricks, strategies, and manipulation.

These disconnection scenarios are problematic because they are sacrificial plays of the worst kind. They manipulate the child, putting their greatest need on the line in the name of desirable behaviour. As these scenarios play out over the course of days, weeks, months, and even years—in ways both big and small—the effects can add up. This is particularly troublesome when we consider that neuro-imaging studies have shown that, at the brain level, the experience of relational disconnection is akin to that of physical pain.[15] But it's just as important to understand that you cannot permanently wreck your kid with a few minor transgressions (more on this later). Keep in mind and take to heart that there is *always* a way to repair through a heightened focus on connection and the championing of healthy, normal development.

You cannot, however, give to your child what you did not get in your own childhood—unless you are willing to acknowledge those gaps and work to fill them in. If you were parented from a place of disconnection, as many parents reading this book will have been, this may be the driving force of your own parental impulses. Even if you experienced a primarily positive childhood, it's still possible to suffer from the smaller and larger misses of that experience. If you experienced significant wounding as a child, it could be that the blueprint for how to be a parent may be missing altogether. And if that wounding was subtler in the context of an otherwise healthy parent-child relationship, it's possible that there are some nuanced pieces missing from your parenting code. What does this look like in real life? Here are a couple of dramatic examples.

One father I know lost his father early on in life, and then he lost his mother to her grief (though she did not die, she was not able to see and hear her son because of her grief). Sadly, his mother lost her next partner to a horrific death a few years later. This meant that in addition to having lost two fathers, this man also twice lost his mother to grief. Yet through his journey he awakened and is an incredibly conscious, attuned, and present dad for his lucky children. Another father I know journeyed along a similar path, but he lost his battle with addiction, lost his children's mother to her addiction, and ultimately lost his children when they were placed in foster care. He was unable to awaken. He could not give his children what they needed. If these children were lucky enough to have an adult with a sparkle in their eye and big love in their heart step into their lives somewhere along the way, they would have a chance to develop resilience and heal from all of these losses and ruptures. This is the extraordinary power of attachment.

On the other end of this wounding spectrum are myriad softer scenarios. Many of you had parents who were present and available, but perhaps you were punished with loss of privileges or activities if you didn't do well at school. A common enough approach, but one that taught you that acceptance is contingent on performance. Believe it or not, that lesson has stayed with you—and until you work through that equation of self-worth with goal achievement, you will be held hostage by the fear of failure. And you will likely pass this same belief on to your children.

Whether the wounds are deep cuts or small nicks, it's essential for every parent to understand that we must make sense of them in order to avoid unintentionally handing them down to a new generation. But as you explore and work through these wounds, don't get stuck on the idea of being "wounded." Simply think of wounding as a normal part of being human. And over-identification with what went wrong in your childhood will not serve you or your child. Instead, accept that there is work to do, and that all of it is within your grasp. Parenthood shines a light on the necessity of this work, which will give both you and your child an amazing chance to grow up healthily.

Developmental Awareness

How many times have you sat in a restaurant and watched a child under the age of six receive a scolding for not sitting still during a meal? Or heard a three- or four-year-old admonished for not sharing? Or observed an eight-year-old punished for having a meltdown when asked to take out the garbage? Or witnessed a fourteen-year-old get grounded for freaking out when told they couldn't hang with friends on a Friday evening?

The parental response of punishment and consequence for such actions is not an uncommon occurrence in our world. Yet each one of those examples represents a child with an underdeveloped brain responding exactly as they *should* according to their stage of development. Many of us fall into the trap of expecting a child to absorb and adopt adult behaviour even though the human brain doesn't fully mature until sometime in the mid to late twenties.

That six-year-old fidgeting at the dinner table is incapable of sustained focus and attention; the three-year-old simply cannot share;

the eight-year-old hasn't developed the self-control needed to stay calm in the face of a roadblock like "chores" when what he really wants to do is shoot hoops; and the fourteen-year-old is bound to lose control of his feelings in the face of big emotions. So settle down, big people. Your kiddos are being and doing just what they are meant to be and do along their entirely normal developmental journey.

The trouble is that waiting for development to occur can be bothersome for us big people raising children in a fast-paced world. We try to hurry development along rather than championing it at every point along the way. But children are not small adults, and we cannot force them into adulthood. Self-regulation will look different in a baby, a toddler, and a preschooler. Babies bite because they know no other way to settle their bodies down. Toddlers have tantrums because they are trying to figure out how to become their own person, even as they lack the ability to settle themselves in the face of heightened emotion. Preschoolers shove, push, hit, and don't wait their turn because those behavioural niceties are still a foreign language when they are taken over by a big desire or need. We must respect that children are growing a brain at the rate of billions of neural connections a day. That level of growth will need to continue for years before they have any natural ability to manage their impulses and make "good choices" with some semblance of consistency.

Once, after I presented a workshop, a father told me how his nine-year-old son had been struggling to manage his big emotions in response to disappointing news or requests by his parents to complete chores. Every time the child lost it, his parents would reprimand him for his "bad behaviour" and use behaviourist-inspired strategies such as consequences, timeouts, and removal of privileges. One day, after yet another of these incidents, the father asked his son in exasperation, "What is wrong with you? Why can't you do as you are told and stop reacting like this? I've told you a million times!" In his gorgeous, infinite wisdom, the son replied to his father, "Dad, what is wrong with *you*? You've told me a million times and I still can't do it. Why do you keep telling me the same thing over and over when I *can't* do it?" Nailed it.

You cannot make growth and maturity happen faster by demanding its progression. As David Loyst, a child development specialist who works with children with autism, says, "I've never seen a plant grow faster by pulling on the top of it." Instead of demanding development, a parent's job is to inspire it and champion it. Now recall that connection and attachment are the foundations for healthy child development. When a child is asked to adopt behaviours that are not yet a natural part of their developmental repertoire, that child is forced to reject development in the name of acquiescence so that they can maintain the connection and secure approval from their parent. How many times did this scene play out for you as a child, whether in your home or in a classroom?

Many of us have internalized this scenario, this dance of "do it or else you will pay with a loss of approval, acceptance, or connection." And now we risk recreating it as parents—unless we are willing to bring it to our awareness and work determinedly to sidestep it. We need to understand wholeheartedly how relationship is essential to healthy child development. And we need to simultaneously reject the option of withdrawing attachment and connection from our children in the name of good behaviour or unrealistic developmental expectations. Growth takes time. Development takes time. Building a strong relationship with our children will ensure that this all goes down exactly as nature intended.

Consciousness

Humans have developed the understanding that our minds are who we are (thanks to Descartes, "I think, therefore I am"), that our

A Parent Is Born 35

minds define us and our concrete reality. We can be led to believe that the thoughts we have about what has made us happy or angry or sad or scared, about why someone looked at us a certain way, about why our child did or did not get into the school we wanted them to attend, and indeed about why our children behave as they do, are a reflection of an absolute truth. But to believe that your thoughts are your concrete reality is probably one of the most torturous misconceptions humans experience.

When my son entered the fifth grade he changed to a school an hour away from our home and had to start taking the school bus. He began to complain about the antics of the older children on the bus, who would sometimes tease and use foul language. One day early in the year this behaviour escalated and prompted me to contact the school so the situation could be turned around. Make no mistake: my mama-bear self was out in full force. I was angry!

On the next school day, I drove my son to the parking lot where the bus picks up all the children. I parked so that anyone looking out of the bus windows would be able to see my face. I even rolled my window down to make sure they could see that I was watching. I watched closely as my son got on the bus and started walking toward the middle to find a seat. Then I saw some of the older boys pointing. My son turned back and walked toward the front of the bus, where he took a seat. I nearly leapt out of my car and onto that bus to tell those awful kids that they weren't going to dictate where my son sat, much less say or do any of the other unkind things they'd been up to. I held onto myself, though, trusting the bus driver to manage the situation. All day I told myself stories. All day I played out the exact way I would put those boys in their place once and for all.

At the end of the day my son hopped off the bus and into our car for the ride home. I waited for the right moment in the conversation and did my best to be relaxed as I asked him what was up with the older boys on the bus that morning. He looked at me, confused, and so I explained that I'd seen him walk toward the back and then turn around to take a seat near the front after they pointed at him. And then the most fabulous thing happened. He laughed.

Now it was my turn to be confused. He explained that the boys weren't being mean at all; rather, they were being kind. He said he likes sitting near the front; he gets less motion sick, plus it's quieter. He didn't often get that seat because a younger boy sits there. On that day, however, the younger boy was not on the bus and so the older boys had generously let him know the seat was available, should he want it. Well. How had I so misinterpreted what I saw through the windows of the bus that morning?

The answer is that my perception was distorted. Without any distortion, what I would have seen that morning is my son getting on the bus, the boys pointing, and my son turning back to sit down near the front. The end. True, my son's earlier experiences on the bus had distorted my lens, but the bigger distortion came from my mind, my experiences. In fact, throughout the whole experience, a pre-existing "program" from my subconscious mind was running the show.

When I replay the experience of believing that the older boys on the bus were unkind to my son, I relive feelings of panic, fear, indignation, and shame. I would love to tell you with absolute certainty where those feelings came from, but the truth is I cannot. Perhaps they reflected a previous childhood experience of feeling unsafe around other children, or older kids, or people in a position of power over me. Perhaps they flowed from a time in my childhood when I was in trouble for something, unable to defend myself, and then punished accordingly. Or perhaps it was the result of a buildup of childhood experiences that led me—and perhaps you in your own circumstances—to feel as I did. Here is the important thing to know: the knowledge of where these feelings and thoughts flow from does not have to be crystal clear for you to work through them. You just need to understand that your thoughts are not always grounded in objective reality. And this is where consciousness comes into play.

The subconscious mind is formed by our past experiences. As a result, living consciously requires that we understand that our reactive thoughts and feelings in any given situation, and the resulting behaviours, are going to be a reflection of our past.

In his book *The Biology of Belief*, Bruce Lipton tells us that the subconscious mind is running the show, and at twenty million bits of information per second, no less (the conscious mind can process merely forty bits of information per second.)[16]

Being consciously oriented means bringing the subconscious mind to the surface and making sense of those beliefs with the conscious mind. To be conscious is to deeply understand that when you feel unsettled or upset or angry or sad, those feelings are not purely a reflection of the current situation but are influenced by the experiences you had when your mind was being formed. Most often you won't be able to pin these feelings of upset to a specific event. They may be an accumulation of early experiences, or they may be the result of something that happened when you were pre-verbal, leaving you no known narrative with which to link them. Either way, when you are experiencing a big, loud, overwhelming feeling, know that you will be best served by making sense of that feeling by understanding its links to the forming of your mind.

Where parenting is concerned, the problem with subconscious behaviour is that if you interpret your perceptions and feelings as truthful and use them to guide your responses, you are essentially parenting from the past. You are not responding to life as your grown-up self. Instead, you are responding as your *child self*. And children are not equipped to raise children. To parent as adults, we need to make sense of the workings of our subconscious mind, which is why parents today are being invited to do their own work. Raffi Cavoukian, the celebrated children's troubadour, included "Conscious Parenting" as one of the nine principles of his Covenant for Child Honouring, one that is championed by the Dalai Lama.[17]

We must dive into the feelings that are potentially triggered by day-to-day living and parenting and make the link between these feelings and our formative past. Our next task is to take care of the child within us—that little boy or girl who was misunderstood or not fully seen or not completely heard or who otherwise didn't get their needs met —and reassure our child selves that we see and hear them fully. Until there is connectivity between your adult and child self, you may feel at odds. You may have the unsettling experience of being disintegrated rather than integrated.

Recently, I sat in my office with a mom who was expressing her significant frustration at the mess her children seemed to constantly leave in their wake. She was beside herself, trying to get them to co-operate in keeping their home tidy. I listened to her story and to the long list of things she had tried in an attempt to get the situation under control. She joked that she must have the worst case of obsessive-compulsive disorder I had ever seen. I asked what her home was like when she was young. She described a large family of eight children with parents who were unavailable physically (they were workaholics) and emotionally, in that she and her siblings were more of a nuisance than celebrated beings. She said everything was loud and messy and out of control, and she'd hated that. In the middle of her description her eyes widened. "Oh my goodness!" she said. "It's not them, it's me, isn't it?"

All of her frustration, her frantic efforts for control, and her feelings of desperation harkened back to the time when her mind was forming. And now, responding to her own children from her four-year-old mind, she was feeling the flood of it anew, and mistakenly finding cause in her children's developmentally appropriate behaviour. The trigger occurred in present time, but her panicky, overwhelmed feelings came from her past experience as a panicky, overwhelmed child. The chaos in her childhood home had made this mom feel disoriented and unsafe. She'd been powerless to bring order to the home, and that powerlessness may have been even more frightening than the noise and mess that caused it. It's also possible that she may have been temperamentally more sensitive to disorderly environments than her siblings, which would have made an already stressful home environment downright traumatizing.

As author and Jungian analyst James Hollis says, it is often our narrative about our childhood experiences rather than the experiences themselves that brings us stress in our adult lives.[18] But as an adult, this mom knows now that she is not powerless. Although she can't control everything, she can see to it that her home is functional and the most important things are attended to, even though there may be more mess in the house than she would ideally like. When we allow ourselves room to grow, we can be fully available to the growing of our own children. Thanks to the inevitable organizational upheaval that comes with having children, this mom was presented with a wonderful opportunity to tend to those little-girl experiences within and grow herself up that much more. And with this awareness, she became much more capable of acting as a competent guide for her own children.

Think about your own parents for a moment. Did they do this type of conscious, mindful work within themselves? If they did not, they likely responded as their child selves rather than their grown-up selves when parenting got tricky. In turn, this means it would have been almost impossible for you to come through your childhood completely unscathed. And that one simple recognition presents grown-up you with a fantastic opportunity. The bottom line is this: if we parent as we were parented—and fail to do the work to create consciousness around the process—then we can only bring our child as far as we were brought ourselves. This is truly the most amazing gift that is given to us as parents: the opportunity to recognize clearly what our work is, to do that work, and to grow both ourselves and our children in the process.

Creating a Program All Your Own

If the potential exists to change your programs at a cellular level, then it's also possible to create your own program and eliminate those from the past that no longer serve the interests of you or your children. This requires taking the time to recognize, understand, and work through the programs that are living in your subconscious system; to connect those programs to the experiences in your present-day life that are bringing you stress and upset; and to grow from there.

But we also need to dismantle some of the societal programming surrounding the reason we become parents. One of the most insidious myths new parents face is the notion that becoming a parent is meant to make you happy—that parenting is a gigantic, euphoric, idyllic, heart-warming experience. This myth does not line up with the emotional reality of many new parents, who may be thinking one or all of these things: I will never get this right; my baby doesn't like me; everybody thinks I'm doing this wrong; it's pathetic how scared I am. This internal conflict can force even the most steady and even-tempered individual into their child self and ancestral family programming. Suddenly you are acting like your mother or your father, or even one of your grandparents.

The truth is—and some of you may find this shocking—we do not become parents to be happy. Multiple research studies show that parents are among the unhappiest groups of people.[19] Instead, and unbeknownst to many prospective parents, becoming a parent is a precious invitation for growth that will either gently present itself or smack us in the face, as the need fits. One of the reasons we become parents is to finally get the chance to grow up ourselves. But the task of growing up is not for the faint of heart. It takes commitment and grit and a massive sense of humour and humility. The American scholar Joseph Campbell made this same point about marriage:

"I think one of the problems in marriage is that people don't realize what it is. They think it's a long love affair and it isn't. Marriage has nothing to do with being happy. It has to do with being transformed, and when the transformation is realized it is a magnificent experience."[20] You can apply the same ideas to becoming a parent.

Know that you can change the story about challenging parenting situations while simultaneously accepting their difficulty. It's a universal truth that parents of babies and young children may not get as much sleep as they are used to. If you find yourself in this boat, you have two choices. You can think to yourself: "I am so exhausted! I cannot cope!" Or you can turn over this negative mantra in your mind and say instead: "My body will do for me what it is supposed to do, and I am grateful for visits with my baby in the quiet of the night." Maybe your toddler is having a lot of meltdowns. Do you choose to think, "I cannot believe that on top of everything else I now have to deal with an unruly toddler!" Or will you choose to think instead, "I love his ferocity of spirit"? Part of being an adult is to fully own your reality and to know that you have created it with your thoughts—the good and, yes, the bad. But more important is to fully embrace the idea that if you don't like a thought, if your story isn't working out for you, you can choose a different one. Parenting is not about waking up every day bathed in happiness; it's about waking up every day fully alert to and immersed in the living of life. Understand that making sense of your own experiences of being parented will be essential to growing up yourself, and your child, in the best possible way. Through time, openness, and hard work, you will land on a universal truth: the best way to make sure that your child turns out okay is to let that little person inside of you grow up into the adult they were meant to be. This is the greatest gift of parenthood—the invitation to create a program all your own that allows for equal-opportunity growth in parent and child. Wow. Thanks, kid!

2

THE BABY BOND

WHEN A BABY is born, it comes into the world knowing that the first priority is to find you. The new babe's eyes open and immediately begin to scan the environment in search of you—her best bet for survival. She cannot see well yet, but her brain is wired to find your eyes. And as soon as she lands on your gaze, she will stop scanning. That's when the magic happens. Well, it isn't really magic, but years of evolution that have perfected this synergistic connection. When that newborn finds your eyes, she will invariably hold the gaze for as long as she can. And as she does you will find it all but impossible to look away. Biologically, fireworks are going off because your brain is bathed in oxytocin. Long known as the bonding hormone, oxytocin connects parent (male or female) to child, chemically and emotionally, setting the stage for a relationship that will be the ultimate determinant in a child's health, well-being, and success in life.[1]

Here is some great news: parents are wired to be good at this, and so are babies. A newborn knows enough to recognize the difference between breast pads soaked with her mother's milk and those soaked with another mother's milk when they are placed on either side of her head; she will naturally orient to the breast pad soaked with her mother's milk. No special training needed. No psychological support required. What a brilliant way to start!

From the first hours of life a newborn is wired to mimic a parent's facial expressions. If you stick your tongue out at your baby or you open your mouth wide repeatedly you might find that she starts to do the same. To put into perspective how incredible this is, keep in mind that your newborn won't have command of her muscles and movements in a determined way until many weeks down the road. It is a reflex, like blinking in bright light. This mimicry also underscores some basic rules of social psychology: that "birds of a feather flock together" and "imitation is the highest form of flattery." We tend to like people who like us, and we determine that they like us when they appear to endorse the similarities between us.

From the first moments of life your baby is on a mission to make sure that you like her and think she's the smartest baby in the land—and she doesn't even know what she's doing! Even though she has no cognitive control over this copycat impulse, your baby will instinctively try to make herself more like you to assure your acceptance. Again, no special training or psychological support required.

Parents are biologically wired too. If you are breastfeeding, you will experience a milk let-down in response to your baby's cry. At night, when she cries out, you may find that you are up and awake with her in your arms before you even know what's happened. You may find that the advice to let your baby cry herself to sleep, or to let her sort herself out before moving quickly to tend to her, doesn't feel right. You may even find it difficult to be away from her at all, especially in the early days. This is nature's way of nurturing the all-important connection between parent and child. In some cultures, it is "mandatory" that the parent, usually the mother, stay at home with the newborn for a full thirty days after birth. During this time, the mother is well taken care of by her family and friends and is released singularly to the task of caring for her new babe.

Now, consider this: *nature wastes nothing.* A newborn baby is biologically wired to pursue and cement connection with a parent, and most parents are wired to take care of this connection instinctually. So don't be afraid to dive headfirst into this burgeoning new relationship and ignore the misinformation trickling in from other influences that may tempt you to overlook your parenting instincts. Everything about child development, and the human condition in general, hinges on the actualization of the attachment relationship, and it becomes the primary focus from the earliest moments of life. Whether they realize it or not, parents will spend most of their energy encouraging and fostering this bond with their children.

This primary relationship—the parent-child connection—forms the entire foundation of what it takes to parent right from the start. A human is not simply a biological entity but a "being" wired to see and to be; to be intelligent and empathic; and to attract, recognize, and participate in the dance of social connection. As a social species, we cannot survive in the absence of connection. And a sweet, new babe already knows this with her breath, with her heart, and with her wise, intuitive soul.

A wonderful dance is taking place in each moment with your newborn, one that weaves the two of you together in your developing relationship. It is so present and so natural in its emergence that you might not even realize it is happening. You are doing this. And whether or not you know it, you are really, really good at it. Remember that you don't need to be taught how to do this; you simply need to allow yourself to fall into your child's very natural invitation to be a facilitator of this relationship.

Think of the moments over the course of each day—and night— that are filling up your baby's relationship cup. When you are feeding your baby and you return her gorgeous gaze, that is a drop in the cup. When she smiles at you and you smile back, another drop is added. When she starts to coo and you respond with a coo of your own—in goes another. When she shows signs of fatigue, like turning her head away or becoming fussy, and you respond with rocking and soothing, you are adding more. When you are changing her diaper and murmuring sweet-nothings, her cup grows fuller still. And when you have skin-on-skin tummy time and your little love hears your heart and feels your warmth, another droplet—or more. Your baby's connection cup will be overflowing within minutes or hours, never mind the abundance in connection that can be created over the course of a whole day.

The key to allowing this relationship to take root is to avoid the urge to look for giant signs of connectedness or to wait for the next telltale wave of warm fuzzies. Rather, it is about being present, moment to moment, for the minutia of the relationship dance. You won't always see neon-sign evidence of it unfolding, but rest assured that it is happening. As certainly as you breathe, the relationship blooms. This is where a little faith comes into play. When you can trust that nature knows its way, that without even understanding what is happening or how, the relationship will flourish, you are able to release yourself to the magic of the dance—that perfected-by-evolution, synergistic magic of the parent-baby bond.

Even with all of your best intentions, it can be seductively easy in our outcome-focused world to measure your progress in creating a healthy relationship with your baby by exhaustively assessing if they are developmentally on track in other ways. Is your baby getting enough tummy time? Should she be lifting her head by now? Is she developing a flat spot on her skull from spending too much time on her back? Is she growing enough, sleeping enough, eating enough? So much tracking and measuring and thinking! Although you of course need to be aware of these sorts of things, I encourage you to focus on feeling and fuelling the connection in ways that feel natural. Allow this wonderful time getting to know your new little person to unfold without being hijacked by thoughts of whether she's met all the milestones. Connection is *the* foundation to healthy growth and development. With that connection underway, those measurable outcomes all but take care of themselves.

The Science of Connection

Before I explain exactly how this deeply connected relationship works in a baby's development, let's consider the history of attachment theory, and the significance of attachment to healthy child development as understood in the scientific literature. As we explore these topics, you'll get a sense of how deeply attachment theory departs from that of the behaviourists discussed in chapter 1.

In a nutshell, behaviourists landed on the logic that if you deprive a child of connection at any age, desired behaviour will result: a baby left alone appears to figure out how to fall asleep; the child who is timed-out appears to behave better. Who among us isn't going to be tempted by parenting "strategies" that result in a better-behaved child who sleeps through the night and performs as expected? The goal of these practices is to ensure desired behaviour on the part of the child—behaviour desired *by the adult*. But why do children respond to them? Be forewarned: the answer to this question may bring you to your knees. A child instinctually knows that without connection they are doomed, so most children will fall into line to secure the connection they desperately need to grow as nature intended.

The understanding of the importance of connection between children and their primary caregivers comes to us primarily via British psychoanalyst John Bowlby's work. When Bowlby was doing research in a hospital during the 1940s, he noticed that young children dropped off at the hospital to receive care appeared to become more ill rather than improving in health. He also noticed that when their parents came for visiting hours the children would appear much improved. Experimenting with these discoveries, Bowlby established that parental presence led to faster improvements in health and far less distress for the child. Not only did this revolutionize hospital practices in terms of parental rooming-in and increased visitation, but it was also seminal in terms of how we understand the inner workings of the parent-child relationship. Bowlby's observations resulted in a lifelong course of research for him and his then student, Mary Ainsworth.

In the late 1960s, Ainsworth designed the paradigm called the "strange situation," used to study attachment theory in the parent-child relationship. Ainsworth placed young children in a series of variously stressful and structured physical separations and reunions with their parents to observe the children's reactions. Through Bowlby and Ainsworth's work it became clear that the nature of the parent-child relationship is significant for positive developmental outcomes. In the 1970s, it was developmental psychologist Dr. Edward Tronick who studied the parent-child relationship using *emotional* separations and reunions. To do this, Tronick devised the still-face paradigm. Tronick asked parents in a controlled situation to interact with their babies face to face as they normally would at home. The parent was then instructed to turn away, wipe her face of all emotion, and then turn back to her baby with a completely "still" face. The still face is devoid of all emotion and connection and appears robotic.

This dynamic was played out with children of different ages, and Tronick observed that, regardless of age, the children noticed immediately the presence of the still face and would become unsettled by it, even very young babies. After keeping the still face for two minutes, the parent was instructed to re-engage with the child in a way that was typical to their relationship. A child used to a responsive caregiver (that is, one who experienced secure attachment) was more likely to settle relatively quickly. The child who was used to a non-responsive caregiver might continue to be unsettled for a long period of time or might not even notice the parent's re-engagement.

You can see how this paradigm works in one disturbing video of a still-faced parent interacting with a three-month-old baby. As the parent continues with the still face, the child becomes increasingly dysregulated and upset. After only two minutes of emotional separation from his parent, the baby turns his head to the side and vomits from distress. What would it be like, then, for a child who experiences this type of emotional separation in an enduring way, as part of the relationship in which they are raised? What parents can learn from these studies is that while simple physical proximity is essential to the provision of care for young children, emotional closeness is also vital if the child is to grow and develop as nature intended.

Secure attachment is the natural state of the parent-child relationship, and what we are wired up to engage in without instruction. But our modern lives feature numerous distractions, some of which can have us unintentionally exposing our babies to a robotic still face. Think of all the moments of opportunity for connection that existed before the invasion of screens and phones. Dr. Kristy Goodwin addresses this in her book *Raising Your Child in a Digital World*, in which she notes that feeding time is incredibly important for the cognitive and visual opportunities it grants babies around facial mapping—an important part of social development. "Brexting," or feeding while texting, interrupts that process. Without a phone and social media and text messages to pull you away, you fall naturally into eye-gazing and gentle murmurs while feeding your baby. Public health campaigns have recently been developed to let parents know that being emotionally attentive to your feeding baby is key to their healthy development.[2] There is no app for your lap!

This provision of physical and emotional contact and closeness for our children is particularly important in the formative early years of their lives. Psychologist Dr. Gordon Neufeld has woven together a large amount of research in the field of child development to map out exactly how the attachment relationship plays out in these early years.[3] He tells us that a baby's first year is characterized by attachment through the senses; that is, a baby makes sense of the connection that is forming primarily through *being with* the parent. The child needs to see, taste, touch, smell, and hear you to know that you are his best bet, that you've got him, and that you can be counted on.

Clearly, the attachment relationship is a foundational piece of growing up our children in the best possible way. This marks a huge shift from the days of behaviourism, the parenting strategies which are, at heart, all about using the deprivation of connection to control a child's behaviour. Attachment theory approaches the growing up of children as developmentally rooted in the creation and nourishment of connection. It also allows parents and other adults to see that each baby and child is exactly perfect in their imperfection. Challenging behaviour and the chaos of childhood are indications that everything is unfolding in exactly the right way. Don't fret about the mess or the noise your baby is making—your biggest focus must be on you and your ability to protect that parent-child connection.

Children must be able to trust the "dance" of reciprocity in the relationship with their parents. Psychologists refer to this dance of trust as "serve and return." A child puts out a bid (usually a cry or some form of behaviour), and the parent responds over and over again. If a baby is left to cry, they will eventually fall asleep because they are exhausted from the stress. Though the baby may reflect the behaviours the parents desire, the internal experience is one of continual angst that ultimately thwarts development. Alternatively, if a parent responds consistently, the baby learns to trust in the certainty of that parent's response. And, if handled as needed, also learns to trust in the goodness of the parent's response.

First, the child truly gets the message that they matter. When the dance of trust and reciprocity between parent and child is consistent, the child develops the belief that they are worthy of love and that they can simply lean into a parent's enduring embrace—physically and emotionally—to receive that love. Over the years, this consistent provision of love from the parent morphs into a consistent provision of self-love from within the child. And the greatest gift a parent can give a child is to help them grow into an adult full of self-love.

Second, as well as learning they can trust their parents to respond repeatedly in a caring way, the child begins to develop the capacity for self-regulation. This is a simple and simultaneously complex manifestation of neuroplasticity. Neuroplasticity is the brain's openness to external influence—that is, the experiences a baby has in the child-raising environment will shape how their brain is growing. A baby's brain gets fired up out of a need for food, for a diaper change, for comfort, for anything. When a parent responds and settles the baby, they are in turn settling the baby's brain. As this happens again and again, a baby's brain learns to hang onto the neural pathways that are repeatedly reinforced and fired up through their parents' ongoing caregiving. Brain fires up. Brain gets settled. Over and over. Those pathways are precisely the ones that will allow a child to become capable of self-regulation, self-soothing, and self-control—eventually. It will take years of the connection dance playing out with consistency for this to unfold. And what predicts how well a child learns to regulate? That depends on how well the parent uses their "own arousal level to counterbalance and/or complement that of the child."[4]

Children will be and do exactly as they are meant to be and do for their own growth trajectory. Our role as parents is to promote our child's development rather than create circumstances or conditions that get in the way of it. When children don't get the connection they need they cannot be released fully to their developmental pathway.

The child who must hang on, claw or grasp at, seek frenetically, or pursue connection with panic is the child who struggles. This is the child who redirects all of their developmental energy to securing the connection rather than striding forward with zest and confidence.

Relief comes for the child who is invited to *lean on* and *rest in* the care of their big people, and this is completely within our realm of control as parents to manage. Though we can occasionally get in the way of healthy development by imposing our own programming on our child's growth, we can absolutely right ourselves in the face of challenges that might otherwise thwart our well-intentioned journey.

Nature Does Not Demand Perfection

Knowing how essential connection is for a child's development, I can understand how new parents might feel overwhelmed or uneasy. This kind of commitment is not to be taken lightly. But guess what? Nature does not demand perfection. Parents do not have to keep up the connection dance constantly and flawlessly. Nature is far savvier. Child development experts coined the term "the good enough parent"[5] to describe a parent who has engaged in the dance of connection well enough that the child has received what is needed, even if it wasn't perfectly delivered all the time.

In his work, Dr. Tronick showed that parents are perfectly in sync emotionally with their children only about 30 percent of the time. The rest of the time, parents are either falling out of sync or finding their way back to being in sync. He calls this falling in and out "the good, the bad, and the ugly." The good is when a parent is on top of the reciprocity of the serve-and-return dance. The bad is when a parent has dropped the ball but is working their way back to being in sync. Tronick believes that this falling out of sync is not the worst thing that can happen because the child does learn that reparation and resolution are possible and real. The ugly is when the parent connection is entirely absent and there is no move toward repair. In this scenario, the child is stuck in a horrible place of disconnectedness.

Bear in mind that when a child has a relationship connection with more than one key caregiver—a mom and a dad, for example—the flavour of each connection is specific to the individual relationship. This means that a child will have a specific connection relationship with mom, a different one with dad, and additional connection relationships with any other caregivers. No one relationship will be quite like the other. However, though the other relationships certainly matter, the one that is most intense and most frequent will be the front-row influencer in terms of the child's development.

And here's another thing to keep in mind: it really does only take one! Many parents come to me full of angst about an absent, uninvolved, or perhaps incapable co-parent, concerned about how this might affect their children. Yes, there will be an emotional impact of some kind. But if a child has at least one adult who is full of invitation for that child to exist, who is delighted to see them when they walk into a room, who has a twinkle in their eye and love in their heart for them, who will absolutely have their back through thick and thin, this is a child who will be okay. Resilience will abound and that child will thrive exactly as they were intended to.

Eventually other caregivers will be invited into your child's inner circle—here is the glimmer of light at the end of the tunnel for all exhausted parents out there! Sometime around the age of two years, your child will start to develop meaningful relationships with others with whom she has ongoing connection experiences. As these other caregivers are invited into your child's inner circle, parents continue to be the most important influence in terms of the child's sense of self and her brain's networks to facilitate self-regulation.

As a rule, the relationships that will have the most impact on the child are those that are (1) most intense; and (2) most frequent. In almost all cases, that relationship is with a parent. If you are an adoptive or foster parent, this is an important message for you to internalize. Though the relationship rupture caused by the loss of the biological parent will be keenly "felt" by a child at the cellular level, the enduring influence on her will be the foster or adoptive parents, as they are her most intense and frequent source of relational interaction.

Clearly, foster and adoptive parents won't be starting from neutral ground. By definition, an adoptive or foster child comes to their new parents in a space of disconnection and loss rather than being bathed in connectedness from the start. It will take time and consistency to make headway. As development carries on, the adoptive or foster child may play out the loss again and again as they make sense of it at this new developmental level of understanding. Extraordinary patience will be needed in this situation, but progress will happen. Even if growth isn't immediately apparent on the surface, there is a rich, underground world of internal growth taking place—trust me.

Nourishing Connection

When my clients want to figure out why their seven-year-old is so anxious or why their fourteen-year-old is cutting (self-harming), I ask questions about the attachment relationship during the first two to three years of the child's life. Many times, what emerges are stories of ruptured attachment, such as a situation in which a parent was unexpectedly hospitalized and thus separated from their child, or the child had to endure invasive medical procedures or was hospitalized for a long period. Sometimes career demands or an intense work schedule can take a parent away from the relationship. Or perhaps issues with a sibling can lead a parent to significantly redirect their attention and presence.

Occasionally, when I ask a parent about the child's early relationship history, a dismissive, even defensive tone may creep into the response—"Well, he was just a newborn when that happened. Surely that isn't relevant," for example, or, "She was so little when that happened; she can't have remembered it." While it is true that a baby will have no concrete memory of these early upsets, and will not ever develop a verbal narrative of the occurrence, the upset lives on in the baby's neurons.[6]

This neurological encoding acts as a sort of memory for the experiences that surrounded the baby at the time of the traumatic relationship rupture. His body encodes sensations, experiences, environments, and other "triggers" that relate back to the experience. Even if he is currently in a safe, solid, connected place emotionally, he can be thrown back into an alarm-ridden state. His neurons hold the memory of the events surrounding the trauma, including body sensations and other things in the environment. Any present-day situation or feeling that reminds him of that time can send him into a state of anxiety. How intense those sensations are will depend on an indefinable and complex equation that considers the child's temperament and level of sensitivity, the presence of any buffering factors, including a safe and connected caregiver, and whether the experience is repeated or compounded by other experiences.

We can never take blissful refuge in the belief that babies don't remember traumatic relationship ruptures. At the cellular level, they do. And unless the distressing event is understood and responded to, it will continue to live on in them in ways that can influence their physical and emotional development, their academic and vocational success, and the ways in which they create and nourish relationships with the important people in their life.

It is much easier to right these kinds of upsets when a child is young because the brain is in a period of explosive growth. With a baby, the emotional story simply needs to be written—not rewritten. But even as a child gets older and eventually becomes an adult, it is still possible to rewire the brain to be more settled; that ability is a reality at any age. The psyche can adjust to a new reality of belief that the world is safe, and the person in question can come to trust that they are worthy. The older one is when this process starts, however, the longer it will take. This is because the brain is no longer growing explosively, and because the story that needs to be rewritten is much more entrenched.

There are so many opportunities to ensure a rich experience for that explosively developing brain and that wonderfully emerging story. The challenge is that capitalizing on these opportunities often means standing in opposition to much of the popularized child-raising culture. I invite you to stand strong in your sense of self as a parent, and to embrace the fact that your priority is to operate in the service of your growing child, and not in the service of that broader cultural dynamic. Think about how you can show up to reinforce the connection relationship you have with your child, rather than doing what feels more convenient or wins greater approval from the adults around you.

Say you have a baby who just doesn't seem able to stop crying. What should you do? Do you buy into the idea that you should put your baby down in her crib and let her figure out how to stop crying? Or, with an understanding of the foundational importance of connection, do you have confidence in the knowledge that it doesn't matter if your baby calms or does not. What *does* matter is that your baby experiences you being there for her. Let her feel you and smell you and hear you while she wails away. Let her know that the connection is strong, and that nothing can get in its way.

Or perhaps you are being encouraged to get your baby onto a feeding schedule so you can get more sleep and your baby can figure out the rhythm of her day. How do you handle this? Again, choose to land on connection. What your baby needs more than anything is to know that you can sense her needs, and upon doing so, will be consistently moved to respond to them. With connection firmly in place, you will feed your baby when she is hungry. It isn't about schedules. It's about presence and provision.

When It All Feels Too Much

As children call out—whether via a cry, a shout, a hit, or a melt-down—a parent's job is to ensure that that child falls into a trust-filled dance of connection. Children must know that when they call, a parent will answer, almost without fail. This is especially true for a baby. For this reason, every single cry from a baby should be thought of as an urgent need. Yes, you read that right: every single cry. Even knowing that it's not necessary to be perfect, and that it takes just one parent to get this right, a baby's needs can sometimes feel overwhelming.

So what do you do if you find yourself feeling overwhelmed? Or struggling with the sense that everything is too intense, too impossible? Or worrying that you aren't good at this, that you will fail, that your baby doesn't even like you, that others think you aren't good at this? Take a deep breath and understand that you have been tripped back into your own childhood programming. Perhaps *your* connection needs were not met in the way you needed them to be. And now, when your baby needs you, that need triggers a huge emotional response.

Sometimes it can feel like no matter what you do as a parent, it just isn't working, it just isn't good enough. And this can bring you to the point of breakdown. If you allow yourself to persist in this negative thinking, you could spiral into a vortex of despair, self-deprecation, or angst, and end up in a terrible space that might lead you to physically or emotionally harm your baby. Shaken baby syndrome is just one potential outcome when parents or caregivers don't step away and take a moment when it's needed.

If you find yourself at this point, it is vitally important that you shift focus from connectedness with your baby to connectedness with yourself. Take a few moments to care for yourself or, if possible, find someone to step in. Make sure your baby is physically safe, in a crib or playpen, and go take some deep breaths. Stepping away is certainly the lesser of all evils here. Once you have regained your true capacity to be available to your baby, you can step back in as a caring adult. Any break in connection your baby may have felt can be repaired as you lovingly reconnect and reassure.

If this happens to you, know that it isn't your grown-up self that is struggling here. It is the smaller, child versions of yourself that have leapt to the forefront and are now controlling the show. Reassure your child self—with a good dose of swagger—that you've got this. You are in charge; you are capable; you are present. Feel that child self come to rest, and then step in once again to your role as capable caregiver.

Sometimes your programming can take over to the extent that you feel utterly unable to escape it. This is when postpartum depression can settle into place. You feel stuck. You feel hopeless. You feel incapable. You might even feel unworthy. This is a devastating place for any parent to land, especially when you probably dreamed for so long of the bliss that parenting would be. If you are in that place, take heart in the knowledge that you are not crazy, and you are certainly not alone. Your experience is real and all too common.

There is a path out of postpartum depression, though it is multi-layered. Do you have wounds from your own childhood that require additional nurturing so they can be healed? Are you carrying an intergenerational wound that has been ripped wide open by your experience of becoming a parent? Or do you need to find ways to care more for yourself so that you can be available to the ultimate role of growing up your baby? You are not wrong to think of yourself. You are not wrong to put yourself and your needs first. You are not wrong for feeling any of the things that might be real for you right now. Yes, your baby needs you. But you need you too. And what is for your greatest good will in fact be for the greatest good of all.[7]

Many parents, especially women and mothers, have absorbed the odd socialized belief that we must put the needs of others before our own. In truth, nothing could be more problematic. Parenting educator David Loyst says, "When I care for myself, I feel self-full and then I notice that I am much more self-less. When I don't care for myself, I find that I need others to behave in particular ways so I don't feel stressed, which is actually being more self-ish." This means that the most central act of service a mother can give to her family is to take care of herself. A mother who does this also, by default, heals, tends to, and takes care of her entire family. You are worth it, Mama. Know that with some gentle guidance, self-care, and consistent personal growth work, you will find a way through.

THERE IS NO such thing as too much comfort, love, and attachment. The idea that you can spoil a child with too much connection is crazy talk. But there *is* such a thing as an anxious parent who smothers from a place of insecurity. The strength of your bond isn't about how often you fuss over or check on your baby. And it certainly isn't about occupying all of your baby's attention or pursuing signs of their affection for you. Instead, it is about consistently answering your baby's call, and trusting their natural development to progress without any pushing.

Unfortunately, our current parenting culture often has us believing the exact opposite; that is, this culture suggests parents are supposed to toughen up their little humans and get them ready for the real world. But the job of parenting is not to grow children who are hardened. Rather, it is to grow children who are hardy, resilient, and who will contribute to making the world a better place—a place that operates from love and compassion rather than from fear and reaction.

Attachment is the birthplace of humanity. It is not mollycoddling; it is science. It is not a tree-hugger, hippy-dippy parenting philosophy for softies; it is life. It is the kind of life where you move in to scoop up your littles and invite them to exist. A life in which parents give children not just the love that they want but the love they need. A life where you fulfill the child's need for belonging, significance, love, and being known. Where there is not only a twinkle in your eye for them but also a twinkle in your heart. Where the resounding energy of your presence in your child's eyes says, "Welcome to the world, my sweet child, I am so glad you are here," day in and day out, with a force that only a parent can muster. A life in which parents accept with full understanding the truth that "you are not managing an inconvenience, you are raising a human being."[8]

3

HOW TO GROW A BRAIN

WHEN YOU PARENT in your most evolved adult self you are available to your child in an energetic presence as much as a physical one. If parents make themselves available through presence—being grounded, aware, seeing—and through responding, connecting, and providing over the many moments in a child's life, a child's brain grows in a way that allows them to become capable of self-regulation; that is, they will be capable of self-control, self-soothing, managing their impulses, and tending to their most dramatic feelings. The crux of parenting right from the start is to create the conditions necessary for nature to do its work.

I recently spent a day on vacation poolside. I landed in my deck chair in the early morning hours when all the young families were already up and about with their wee ones, looking for some water-filled entertainment. On this particular morning, two families descended on the pool. The first included a mom who already looked at her wits' end, even though the day was just getting started. She had a two-year-old son and a daughter, around the age of four, in tow. Her husband briefly buzzed by to say hello, but otherwise she was on her own. The shrill quality of her voice—not to mention the constant narrative streaming from what had to be an extremely anxious inner mother ("Don't do this, do that... if you don't I will... stop that... no touching...")—attracted the attention of everyone around the pool. On and on it went. The woman's daughter obviously wanted to make sure her mama was happy, and part of achieving that goal was to keep her little brother under control. There was no rest for this little girl. As for the little boy, he was acting exactly his age. Two-year-olds are all about becoming their own person. He wanted to go and do and jump in the pool and throw rocks from the garden into the pool, and... and... and... His mom was beside herself with frustration and resorted to putting him in one timeout after another. She would plop him down on his little bum in the middle of the pool deck and force him to sit still. Every time he tried to get up she would tell him what a naughty boy he was and threaten to take them all straight back to the hotel room if he committed any of these heinous acts again. His older sister looked on in horror. It was clear that she loved the pool and desperately wanted to stay, so she worked harder to keep Mama happy and her little brother in line.

Enter family number two. This group also had two children, but slightly younger—a baby around six months of age and a three-year-old boy. Grandma and Grandpa were both on deck, alongside Mom and Dad. Dad was trying to get some work done on his computer, so he was mostly unavailable, but he did have a beautiful way of responding to his son's bids for attention. When the little boy called out, "Papa—look at me—I'm swimming," his dad would respond with, "I see you, my boy—look at you," and then get back to work. The baby didn't like the water, so Grandpa stepped in to take him for a walk in the gardens. Grandma and Mom splashed about in the pool with the little boy. Like the boy in the first family I observed, this little guy was in the throes of becoming his own person—he wanted to go and do and see. But he was given a slightly longer leash than his counterpart, and there was far less anxious energy floating in the space between him and his caregivers. Like the first little guy, this one also stepped out of bounds and had to be reminded of the limits. But he was reminded in the gentlest ways—with quiet and strong eyes from his mama, and a kind but firm reminder from his grandma. In between these reminders, he was bathed in the attention of his big people as the moment and situation called for. The energy about him was palpably different than the energy around the first little boy.

This story is not about how many caregivers were present and on deck, although I do acknowledge that not every parent will have a wonderful range of built-in support like the grandparents travelling with the second family. This story is an illustration of how the kind of parental energy a child experiences during their first years will have a lasting impact on brain growth. Now remember, I'm not talking about an off day here and there. In fairness, that first mother was having a stressful day and may have needed a break, which simply wasn't available to her. This happens to all parents, new and experienced. What I am referring to is the cumulative, day-to-day experiences of childhood that influence a child's growth, whether optimal or not.

To see how this might play out, let's advance the developmental clock about three years, to a point when each of these little boys arrives in a school classroom. I am clearly taking some liberties with the following forecasts, but my clinical experience tells me that children who are continually surrounded by anxious energy, like the little guy with the overwhelmed mama, will likely struggle. He may present with scattered attention born of this anxious energy, for that is what he is marinated in. He may struggle to regulate himself and will need constant reminders from adults and others to adhere to the social and classroom rules. He may even be labelled with behaviour problems or diagnosed with attention deficit hyperactivity disorder.

The other little guy? He will likely have a greater capacity for internal regulation, as he has been regulated peaceably, compassionately, and gently by an exceptionally present host of big people. He has been nurtured in calmness, which may present in his behaviour as a capacity for more impulse control and self-regulation. His neurons have been allowed to practise this self-regulation repeatedly because of the gentle nature of the caregiving he was provided.

The Brain Bridge

Two things to know: (1) children are not born with the capacity to self-regulate, and (2) the human brain is the only organ that is regulated fully from the outside. Psychiatrist Dr. Daniel Siegel says that "coherent interpersonal relationships produce coherent neural integration within the child that is at the root of adaptive self-regulation."[1] What this means for children is that instead of having a full grasp of how to modify emotions and regulation (being and feeling settled) from within, they seek regulation outside of themselves. They are first regulated within the context of their most intense and frequent relationships, and only then, through this experience, do they develop the capacity to self-regulate.

One of the basic principles of neuroplasticity is that "neurons that fire together, wire together."[2] The more repetition certain neuronal tracks in the brain have with being fired up in a given sequence, such as those responsible for self-regulation, the more likely those tracks will take root in the brain as a well-functioning system. A child will not learn how to self-regulate if a parent does not first provide opportunities for him to be continually regulated via a safe, emotional connection over and over again so that those neurons start to wire together. When a parent regulates via emotional connection they are creating in their child what neurobiologists call a "brain bridge." When two brains are connected within the context of relationship, the resonance established between them allows, in this case, the child's brain to be settled from the outside by the parent's brain.[3] So use your brain and settle theirs!

This provision of physical and emotional contact and closeness for our children is particularly important in the formative early years of their lives when the brain is developing most rapidly. Parents often ask how they can connect with their child in meaningful ways during these most important years. Psychologist Dr. Gordon Neufeld shines a valuable light on how children make sense of the attachment relationship at different ages, and, in turn, how parents can tune in to that to help those neurons wire up in the best possible way.[4]

Year One: During a child's first year the attachment relationship is understood in sensory terms. Babies want to taste you and smell you and feel you and hear you and look at you. They attach through their senses. This is how they know you are close, how they hold onto the idea of you, and how they are regulated by you. This means that lots of close physical contact between your baby and you, along with his other most important big people, is vital during this period.

Year Two: In the second year of life the child adds to this sensory approach a way of making sense of your connection via the concept of *sameness*. During this period the child will understand the safety of your relationship by observing the similarities between you and him. Mommy likes apples just like me! Daddy has a penis (true story) just like me! Mommy and I love playing in the sand, Daddy and I love cars, and so on. Focusing the spotlight on similarities will be the love language of a child in the second year of life.

Year Three: In the third year your child makes sense of being connected to you through a fierce sense of *belonging and loyalty*. Preschoolers need to know they belong and will show fierce loyalty to that knowledge. They become highly possessive of Mom, which can make the introduction of a new sibling at this stage particularly dramatic, though that doesn't mean the idea is terrible or to be avoided. They also understand the concept of family during this period, and the idea that they belong to a family. Having rituals that only you and your child know—like secret handshakes and ways you say hello and goodbye and using the possessive "my boy" or "my girl" when exclaiming over something they have done—will boost your connection.

Year Four: In their fourth year a child develops a true sense of closeness through *significance*. During this period your child rejoices and feels settled and secure with repeated reinforcement of the idea that they matter. They will seek forms of contact that solidify this understanding for them, including showing you every drawing they do so that you can proclaim how much you love it (over and over again!). To keep their cups running over, think of ways you can be one step ahead of them in repeatedly providing the message, with words and actions, that they are important.

Year Five: It is in the fifth year that the concept and feeling of *love* truly drops into place for your child. Your child will literally and figuratively give you her heart. She will draw you hearts, create heart-shaped crafts for you, paint you hearts, and make you heart cards. And she will legitimately and deeply feel this love in her heart. This is the wonderful stage when your child falls in love with you—a stage misinterpreted by Freud in his thinking about the Oedipus complex, in which he tried, erroneously, to make sense of why children seem to "fall for" one or the other of their parents around this age. Go big with love for your child in the fifth year, as this is the new language of his growing little heart.

Year Six: Although falling in love might seem like the deepest level of attachment your child could have with you, it isn't until their sixth year that your child moves into connection at the most profound level—that of being truly and wholly and profoundly *known*. They understand that the good, the bad, and the ugly of them can shine through in the restful knowledge that all will be accepted and championed. The ultimate message for the child to take away from this stage, one that will follow them for the rest of their days, is "I am worthy, I am loved, I am seen, I am heard." You will know that you've arrived at this place when your child begins to share their secrets with you and looks to you as someone who genuinely "gets" them as a person.

If all goes as nature intended, and a child gets what they need over their first six years, with attachment growing progressively more profound with each passing year, attachment will settle in and take root. If there is a significant trauma that is not ameliorated, big ruptures that are not repaired, or inadequate provision, the process will be interrupted. If the relationship is not righted, the child will likely stagnate at that level for the rest of their life.

It is through relationship that the omnipotent foundation of attachment is laid. Knowing the progression of this relationship formation through the early years can be helpful in making sense of what your child needs from you so that her growing brain, and indeed her growing sense of self, have a chance at being optimally regulated from the outside, and thus developing beautifully. Next, we will look more broadly at how the brain grows and what other conditions can be fostered, in addition to the attachment relationship, so that all is optimally in place for your little one to grow and go.

The Smart Heart

An understanding of how the human brain grows is grounded in science, but perhaps no other human developmental process is utterly impacted by heart—and by heart I mean an environment full of love, compassion, and connection. In the growing of a human brain, heart and science coalesce with synergistic brilliance, and the process is more complex, layered, and involved than a simple understanding of neuroscience.[5] Think back to the story of the two families by the pool. The first mama is reacting from a decidedly different place than the second mama (who I do recognize had some help). So as much as parenting right from the start is about science, it is equally and importantly about the heart of the child's environment.

As we've learned, the infant brain is growing at an explosive rate. Scientists also know that neuroplasticity—the brain's ability to change throughout a person's life as directed by external influences—is inextricably linked to *how* the brain grows. Through neuroplasticity, a child's brain soaks up the world, which means that the direction of a child's brain growth and development is not a predestined, scientifically resolute path. Instead, a child's brain will be hugely influenced by what is happening in the world around them. Siegel proposes that the environment shapes the mind and then the mind shapes the environment.[6]

Knowing this gives a parent the profound power to reach into their baby's brain and influence it in the most incredibly positive way. It simultaneously gives a parent the profound power to influence the child's developing brain in a damaging way. Remember: you don't need to be a *perfect* parent. You only need to be *good enough.*[7] But good enough at what, exactly? You need to be good enough at creating the environment that your child's brain needs as they grow. So yes, you will stumble. You will lose your patience, or need a moment to yourself, or become frustrated because you have done nothing but carry around a fussy babe all day long. And that is okay. You are allowed to be imperfect. Then, you move along, pick up the pieces, dust off, and carry on with righting the relationship, soothing upset, and, yes, growing your babe's amazing brain.

Dr. Bruce Perry is a psychiatrist whose life's work is devoted to understanding what children's brains need to grow in the best possible way. He has figured this out by studying the most tragic of cases in which children received the exact opposite—children who were highly traumatized, horrifically neglected, and/or terrifyingly abused. What is most remarkable about Perry's work, and the work of so many others in the field of child development (including Daniel Siegel, Tina Payne Bryson, Maggie Dent, Laura Markham, and Gordon Neufeld) is that the science of it comes down to those three components that I mentioned at the outset: love, compassion, connection.

In studying what happens when children get the complete and absolute antitheses of what they need, Perry's research with highly traumatized children distilled scientific explanations for how parents can best create an environment in which children can thrive. What follows is my take on Perry's six truths about the human brain. These truths shed important light on how a child's brain growth and the parenting they receive are woven together, and how you can ensure the best outcome for your little one.

From the Bottom Up

Perry's first truth is that the human brain is organized in a hierarchical fashion from the bottom up. Just as the secret to a solid structure is a solid foundation, it is important that the "downstairs" or bottom part of the brain grows steadily and soundly. The downstairs brain houses much of the neural circuitry for emotional responding and control, and is the part of the brain that will be exploding with growth in the early days, months, and years of a child's life. We've learned how crucial relationship and attachment is for a child's development. Given that the current thinking about child development indicates that the environment does indeed create the mind, these early years are the moment for parents (and all other big people) to get it right. As neural connections take root in the base of the brain it is imperative that parents create an environment full of loving connection in which their child's brain can marinate. The focus at this time is not on learning, preparing them for school, or enrolling them in a zillion extracurricular activities to give them a leg up. Rather, the focus is on loving and playing and exploring and growing, all with a foundation of attachment and ultimate trust in nature's brilliant way.

Use It or Lose It

Neural system change is "use-dependent," meaning that the brain takes a "use it or lose it" approach. Whatever neural systems are activated most often are the ones the child's brain will hold onto as more permanently wired into the neural structure of the brain. Neural systems responsible for self-regulation are not exempt from this use-it-or-lose-it tendency toward that permanent wiring. If a child is consistently responded to and calmed with compassion whenever he is upset, hurt, or ill, that child's brain will hold onto the neural systems responsible for self-regulation. But if a child lives in a stressed state because their emotional needs are not being tended to, their brain will hold onto the circuitry that has the child being more practised at being stressed. This will be a brain that has difficulty with self-regulation—a brain that has learned that the world is an alarming place where you cannot be at rest and where you must be constantly vigilant and on guard. The key for parents and other big people to remember is that consistency of response is vital for the growing child. The focus ought always to be on calming and regulating the child first, with instruction and reminders to follow only when the brain is settled and soothed.

One Step at a Time

As mentioned earlier, the base of the brain is the first in the important sequence of development. Every other part of the brain, the physical neural circuitry and the resultant pathways for thinking and problem-solving, builds on top of that foundation. Parenting with consistently and calmly delivered connection, love, and compassion will result in a child with a solid foundation for emotional regulation, one who is more likely to reason effectively and to solve problems. Remember that this is a process that takes time. And steps may be missed when a child does not receive the kind of connection he or she is seeking. When a step is missed in the brain's sequence of development, this hole must be filled before the rest of the brain will be able to grow and thrive. A child cannot leapfrog to a place of well-developed maturity if the brain is missing a step in the growth sequence. If this happens, parents, therapists, or psychologists must assess the child's missing needs, and then go back and help the child grow the neural connections that were missed.

For example, we've learned that in the first year of life, babies understand their developing attachment through their senses. When they are held, rocked, and sung to, amazing growth happens in the foundational neuro-circuitry of the brain. If that holding and rocking doesn't happen, they won't develop the neurological pathways that this would otherwise have created. This can possibly result in lapses in the ability for self-regulation, which in turn might lead to behavioural challenges or mental health issues such as anxiety down the road.

Part of the therapeutic process for a child who has missed out on optimal early caregiving experiences may be to find ways of providing that child and her brain with what was missed. Think touch, rhythm, and sound—a parent, for example, who lovingly rubs lotion into her child's hands and arms, soothingly brushes her hair, invites a linking of arms on a long walk, or connects with their child through the rhythmic sounds of a drum circle. This is the logic behind Perry's Neurosequential Model (NSM) of Therapeutics, and also what is espoused by therapists who understand interpersonal neurobiology. The thing with growing neural connections is that you aren't going to see the results right away. Consistency will be key while you allow nature to do its work and the brain to find its way.

Get a Head Start

The fourth truth is that the brain develops most rapidly early in life. As we've learned, it is forming approximately a million new neural connections per second.[8] Imagine how microscopically small a neuron is. Now consider that during this period of unfathomably explosive brain growth, the infant brain weighs only 25 percent of its eventual adult size. By the time a child reaches their second birthday, their brain will have grown to 75 percent of its eventual adult size. The rate of neural growth in a young child is stunning! With this rapid growth and what experts know about neuroplasticity, it makes deep sense that children's brains are the most open to external influence during this early period in life. The brain is not static but is constantly changing form by responding to its external environment and then coding those experiences internally. As you think about how to set up your child's world, remember your role in ensuring that these early years are calm, consistent, and absolutely full of connection. Sometimes creating such a reality takes a fierce stepping in and a sincere consideration of priorities. I encourage all parents to take some time to figure out how you can do this for your child.

Change is Possible

Neural systems can change, but some are easier to change than others. Not all neural systems are as "plastic" or open to external

influence. Again, nature takes care of business, as it is the foundation or "downstairs" part of the brain that is the most amenable to
change. This is exceedingly important since the foundation must be
built well for the rest of the brain to have a chance to thrive. Everybody knows that the secret to a solid structure is a solid foundation.
And as it happens, that foundation is the base source of self-regulation. So if a young child misses out on the contact, closeness, and
care needed for optimal development of the brain's regulatory core,
this will need to be proactively addressed later through consistent,
attachment-based caregiving.

Countless peer-reviewed studies have shown the remarkable
potential for the brain to change. For example, Megan Gunnar and
colleagues[9] showed that a sample of traumatized children recently
placed in foster care had initial high levels of cortisol in their system. Cortisol is the stress hormone—secreted in times of alarm in
an effort to help your body respond so you can keep yourself safe
through fight, flight, or freeze. A child with a history of maltreat-
ment will likely have adapted by developing a brain that is good at
responding to stress. This kind of response works well in an environment where a child needs to be on alert for the next moment of high
need or attack. However, it also makes that same child susceptible
to stress and anxiety.

What researchers like Gunnar and her colleagues have discovered is that cortisol is actually toxic to the developing brain. But
with the sole intervention of consistent, compassionate, attachment-based caregiving, that heightened response shifted to be
more like the cortisol response patterns of children without traumatic histories. It took three months to make that change, a change
that altered the entire life course for each of those children. As a
rule, the older the child or, indeed, the adult, the longer and steeper
the climb toward change, but the door is never shut entirely. The
amazing thing about the human brain is that it wants to be okay. Scientists have identified something called the "self-righting tendency."

Given half a chance, the brain will push toward recovery and optimal outcomes. And when we're talking about the brain of a child—a brain that is exploding with growth and potential—the likelihood that your responsive caregiving will make all the difference is exceptionally high. So love them and tend to them—and then watch the brain do its thing.

Social by Design

The last of Perry's truths is that the human brain is designed to be social. We are meant to grow in a world of relationships, to be absolutely steeped in connection. In generations past humans lived within more relationship-rich communities and structures than many of us do today. We lived in tribes, and then in villages and multi-generation homes—some families still do! We had built-in structures and systems for parents to be cared for as they cared for their children. We slept, ate, worked, and played together.

Contrast that with how children grow up today: often in small, mobile, nuclear families with both parents working, at a distance from grandparents and other family members, and socialized in homogenous groupings at playdates or programs, daycare centres, and eventually at school. In our fast-paced developed countries, where we focus on success and driving forward in life, one of the most rapidly growing prejudices is ageism. And why is that? Many children spend comparably little time around their extended families, making grandparents and other aging family members unfamiliar and even frightening. Our isolated existence means that children have been distanced from other members of society—so much so that a new prejudice has developed!

Our culture also constantly lumps children in with peers of the same age. Two-year-olds don't need to hang out with other two-year-olds—at least not all of the time—as this does not improve their ability to socialize. Young children are meant to learn social skills from their parents and from older, wiser peers and adults within their "village." Eventually they will learn how to apply those social skills in various and more public settings, like school with their peers.

When children are immersed in a heterogeneous world filled with people of different ages, they are offered the opportunity to observe and experiment with upcoming developmental stages as modelled by older and more competent individuals in a safe and secure environment—and this results in more opportunity for growth. Social by design, and yet few children get to experience the richness of relationship in the way Perry describes. You can gift that richness to your children by not playing to the sanitized, homogenous ways of our contemporary world. Think multi-age groupings of all sorts of people—children and adults. Big family gatherings, involving extended family and grandparents in child-care, avoiding too many group activities of same-aged littles, and every other chance you get to marinate your children in a more tribal, village-like existence—do it! This is what grows social brains for our social species.

THE UNITING THREAD of Perry's six truths is that relationship matters in an unequivocally profound way to every growing baby and child. Relationship is how you grow a brain! If there is one message parents should internalize about how to grow their little humans it is this: children need—not want, but need—to be held in the safe physical and figurative embrace of their most special big person or people. They don't need fancy high chairs and high-tech strollers and the coolest toys. Children need their parents to be present and guiding from their adult selves with understanding, patience, and love. When that happens, the capacity for self-regulation will be nourished and nurtured.

Remember that there is a lot of "keeping the faith" in growing a human brain. The growth you are cultivating will not be immediately discernable. You can't see your child's neurons connecting, and the fruits of your labour often remain undetected for a long time. Parents will spend years cultivating the soil for growth, adjusting the environmental conditions when necessary to provide the right atmosphere and weathering the storms when you cannot. One day you will look at your child and be amazed by the incredible human that is looking back. That human being will reflect all that you have poured into your child. And you will be absolutely, magnificently stunned.

4

WHY PARENTS NEED
TO BE IN CHARGE

M Y YOUNGEST SISTER recently got married. She has a six-year-old bonus daughter from her husband's first marriage. Lucky me, I was assigned hair and tiara-positioning duty for sweet little Chelsea on the day of the wedding. This is possibly the best thing you could ever ask of me (as the mom of two boys, I never get to do that sort of thing in my home!).

I have an unwavering belief in a couple of things: first, I know I have big swagger as an auntie; and second, I am a rock star when it comes to hair and makeup and, of course, tiaras. So it didn't faze me when my sister said, "By the way, she hates having her hair done. I can never get near it with a brush. Good luck!"

On the morning of the wedding Chelsea was dropped off, and she and I began prepping and primping. So little did it concern me that she hates having her hair done that I forgot about my sister's warning. I had no worries that this wasn't going to go well. I didn't say things like "What do you want me to do with your hair," or "What colour of elastic do you want me to use," or "You just let me know if I'm pulling too hard." If you read carefully between the words of those statements, you can sense hesitation and deference.

Instead, I said things like, "I know exactly what is going to be perfect for your hair," and "Pink or blue elastic, my love?" and "That was a little ouch, but here we go, I've got you." Chelsea sat there and loved it. Why? Because I had no self-doubt about how this was going to happen. That is swagger. That is being large and in charge, and never losing touch with kindness.

Later in the evening one of Chelsea's cousins bumped into her as they were playing around, and her tiara was knocked askew. Chelsea burst into tears and a frantic groomsman came rushing over to my table to let me know they were having a tiara emergency. I scooched over to see her while she was in meltdown mode. Crouching down, I was already saying things that would let her feel heard, because that's what big people do when they are truly kind and in charge. They don't minimize or brush off. They step in and see and hear with swiftness and certainty. I said things that stated the obvious, but I said them with compassion—such as, "Oh love, your tiara got knocked" and, as she raged on about her awful, mean cousin, "You don't like it when he makes your tiara go sideways," and "That made you really upset," and "Of course you are angry." Then I started to walk her through the meltdown: "You can be angry. You are allowed. That makes perfect sense," and "I am right here. I know what we will do. I have extra hairpins with me, and I am going to get it sorted out." Within a minute Chelsea's tears stopped. I settled the tiara into place and told her she was gorgeous. A smile replaced her anger, and she darted off to find the cousin that she really likes. I stood up to walk back to my seat and happened to catch the gobsmacked expression on that groomsman's face. As I walked away I heard him say, "That was amazing!" You know what that is? That is swagger. That is being large and in charge.

This is a small-scale example of what kind of energy backs the sort of big person who is full of confidence in guiding their child through life. Your challenge as a parent is to find it within you to bring that sort of energy to the moment-by-moment reality of your little person's everyday world.

Go and Grow vs. Stop and Stagnate

When a child starts questioning whether you are in charge and whether you know what you're doing, your swagger has evaporated. If your child scans their environment and sees that you are wavering, that you are tapping out, that you are exasperated and have run out of steam, that child will not be assured that the situation is going to work out. Instead, they will believe they need to step in and take charge of situations yet to come and, in fact, take charge of their life. And this means, most catastrophically, that they are now in charge of… you.

Put yourself in that child's place for a moment: Imagine you have hired a guide to lead you through the life-threatening but thrilling climb of Mount Everest. Along the way, conditions get harsh. You wonder if you have what it takes to make it. You wonder if you should turn back. You wonder if you should give up. But your guide keeps leading and encouraging you and taking care of you, so you carry on. However, as the challenges increase you notice that they are wearing on your guide. You hear frustration in his snippy retorts, a change in his tone, and you see the impatient look in his eyes. Suddenly, your guide starts to waver on his plan for the ascent. He asks you for advice on how much higher you should climb that day, if you think it is too cold to press on, and which route would be safer. Say what? Who is in charge here?

Sit in that space and think about whether you would be thrilled to be on this trek with this guide. What has his unstable energy and wavering confidence left you with? Do you get the sense that he has abdicated his position as your fearless, capable leader? What are you, the one depending on him, going to do? Are you going to give up, give in, and wait for death? Or are you going to bravely cobble together a plan to get you (and him!) out of this alive? When you take stock of the situation, the terrifying truth is that you are now in charge. How do you feel about that? Is it restful or troubling? Are you at your best or do you feel angst-ridden? This is how a child is feeling and thinking when they sense that you have inadvertently surrendered the leadership role in your relationship to them.

The devastating result of this change in leadership is that once a child has taken the lead it's very difficult to reverse the situation. A child who has been thrust into the lead position in terms of charting their own developmental course is not suddenly going to sit back and think, "Oh, you've got this now? Okay great. I'm just gonna chill out over here," when you decide you want to be the leader again. At this point, it will take a completely attuned and conscious parent to get back in the driver's seat. I tell you this with brutal honesty: the most difficult thing to manage in terms of the parent-child dynamic is trying to take back your lead position after you have surrendered it.

The other reality of this regrettable switch in leadership is that a child who is in the lead will not be in a state of emotional rest and thus cannot go and grow. Instead, this child will summon all of their mental reserves to figure out how to make a go of being in charge. Rather than "go and grow" it becomes "stop and stagnate," and this leads to a child stuck in a state of perpetual immaturity. Think again of the Everest climb. Do you believe wholeheartedly that you are going to make it to the top without a guide? Even if you do manage to summit, will it have been via a route that left you exhilarated when you reached the top or exhausted and unable to enjoy the view? The latter is how it will be for the child left to navigate their own development, unable to rest and lean into the care of their most important big people.

Parents don't have to be perfect to maintain the lead position. You will drop the ball. You will make a wrong call. You will force something that shouldn't have been forced. You will lose your patience. You will yell. You won't be your best self—and probably daily. Taken on their own, these behaviours are not enough to produce a catastrophic demotion in your leadership. The demotion takes place because these behaviours are repeated frequently over time, a pattern that gives your child the message that you aren't on top of this parenting thing. This might happen more quickly if you have a sensitive child. Or if there are big changes happening that could deplete your child's coping resources, such as a household move, a divorce, daycare changes, or the birth of a sibling.

What is most important to recognize is that only the lead person—you—can create the space for your child to take charge, whether you do so directly and with intent or whether circumstances beyond your control generate the change in leadership roles. Regardless, the job of turning it around is on your shoulders. Your "difficult" child did not create this situation. Your challenging life circumstances did not create this situation—even if they may have primed it. Your impossible parenting partner did not create this situation—even if you have all the evidence in the world to suggest the contrary. In the (subconscious) eyes of your child, you created this. That is just how it works. Ouch. I know.

The "A–H" Dynamic of the Parent-Child Relationship

Exactly what does it mean to be in charge as a parent? And what precisely is the nature of the hierarchical structure of the parent-child relationship? The energy of this hierarchy is about inviting your children to lean on you so that as they grow and mature they will find themselves able to stand tall on their own while surrounded by the steadying presence of you and other loving attachments. If you think of this from a visual perspective, the relationship with your child should progress from an A-frame to an H-frame through the years.

The A-H Dynamic

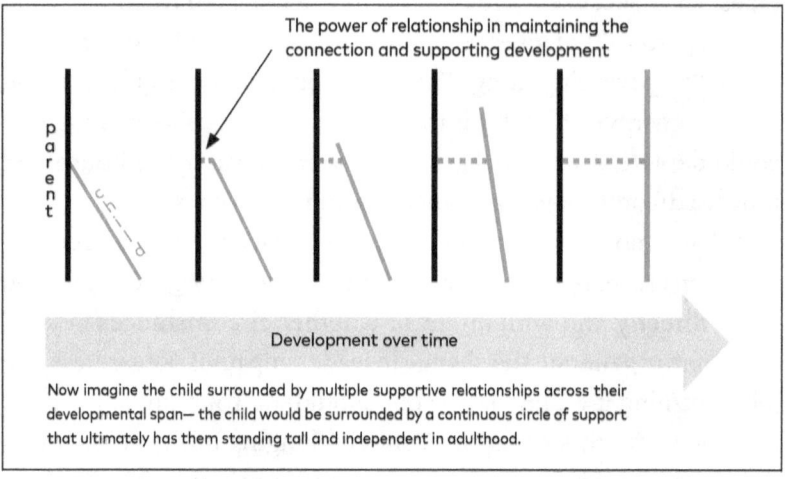

The power of relationship in maintaining the connection and supporting development

Development over time

Now imagine the child surrounded by multiple supportive relationships across their developmental span— the child would be surrounded by a continuous circle of support that ultimately has them standing tall and independent in adulthood.

In the beginning, a parent provides a firm, caring, in-charge presence that the child can lean into. As the child grows, they gradually begin to stand upright. As the child moves toward adulthood, the connection between parent and child continues. Even in adulthood the connection is strong, but instead of the child fully leaning on the parent, the grown child stands with strength, supported by the beam of the H-frame that is the relationship that connects them with their parent. Now imagine that because of the wonderful way you have cared for your child, he becomes able to develop other nurturing attachment relationships, some in childhood and others as he progresses into and through adulthood. Eventually, your child will become surrounded by multiple supportive H-frame relationships across their developmental span that have him standing tall and secure, independent, and capable.

Surrender to Swagger

When you have a clear understanding of how important it is to be in charge and be a safe, nurturing, steady support that your little one can lean into as she grows, the obvious question is: How do you do this? What does it look like and how does it feel? How will it play out in everyday life? How will you know that you've got it? Counterintuitively, if you want to "do" this well, the place to begin is to not think about the *doing* part of it at all. Rather, it comes down to manifesting a certain energy, incorporating a way of BEing so that you can develop and maintain your swagger as the in-charge parent who nourishes trust and connection with your child. Here is how to ensure you are in that lead position and that your child receives the sublime gift of leaning into your capable guidance.

In my book *Discipline Without Damage*,[1] I outlined a three-part mantra to help parents grasp this idea of BEing as the source of DOing when it comes to raising our children. The mantra is: **See It. Feel It. Be It.** The idea is that before you get all locked down in thinking about how you are going to do this, and exactly what it is going to look like, and what three or four or more steps you will need to take to get to the point where you feel you have delivered on this in a measurable kind of way, you first have to feel it. When you are truly feeling what is happening in the moment for your child, you will be beautifully positioned to figure out the next step. You have to create an internal awareness, an energy of swagger, a sense of your innate power to step IN and figure life out for and alongside your child. You can't possibly put the destination before the journey.

SEE IT involves you observing what is happening externally for your child: they are crying, acting out, or having a meltdown. This should take you about a millisecond to establish. The issue is that too much parenting begins and ends with seeing your child's behaviour. You don't like what you see so you respond in a way to make it stop.

Unfortunately, squashing the behaviour doesn't honour your child's developmental needs and serves only to thwart the trajectory of natural growth and development. Instead, it is important to move to the next step.

FEEL IT includes two parts: After reading my first book and attending some of my workshops, parenting educator David Loyst noted that often "you have to feel yourself first, so that you can feel your child." "Feel it," then, is all about what is going on behind the scenes, under the surface, and into the heart—first within yourself and then with your child's behaviour. You must land in an emotional space of feeling for your child, understanding what is happening in that moment and in all the moments that led up to it.

But you can't dive into the business of feeling for your child if you are stuck in your own stuff. Are you embarrassed that everyone is watching your two-year-old have a tantrum? Are you worried that all the people on this plane listening to your crying baby are annoyed and judging you? Are you convinced that your parents or your in-laws think you are handling this moment all wrong, and that they are awful for believing they know better than you? If you have a big story or program playing itself out in your brain in the moment when you are responding to your child, you will be wrapped up in that and will not have the capacity to be understanding of and empathetic to your child's emotions. Sort out your own stuff first.

Let's say your child is losing it in the grocery store. You feel the hot flush of agitation, impatience, embarrassment, and shame rising up inside you. Pause right in that feeling. Acknowledge that you feel anxious or angry. Accept yourself as the parent who feels that. Remind yourself that this is allowed and also that this is about the little child within you feeling freaked out. It isn't a reflection of capable, competent grown-up you. See the little you, even if just for a split second, and have compassion for her. Commit to spending some time thinking through that more deeply—later. Promise yourself that you will give some attention to those fears and feelings coming forward from your child self, and then deliberately turn your attention to your child's emotions instead. You have the brain maturity to choose which thoughts you will feed and which you will set aside. Your child does not. Set yourself aside compassionately for now and instead choose to recognize all that is happening to and inside of your child and extend yourself to them compassionately.

Later, honour the commitment you made to come back to you. Let your compassion for your child feed compassion for yourself. See your own fears and feelings from the perspective of your loving, strong parental self toward your sweet, needy inner-child self. Understand that you were freaking out in the grocery store along with your toddler because you experienced similar feelings of disappointment and frustration when you were small, or perhaps because you experienced similar scorn and judgement from people around you for not being good enough. Recognize that maybe those moments in your childhood were met with disconnection instead of connection. Give recognition and compassion to your child self just as you gave it to your actual child in the moment at the grocery store.

As you engage in self-care moments like this again and again, they do become easier. With practice and commitment it becomes almost second nature to catch yourself feeling triggered by something that is happening with your child or otherwise in your life, neutralize your feelings, and then get down to the business of feeling for your child. Sorting your stuff out is what I call FEEL IT ME, and sorting your child's stuff out is what I call FEEL IT CHILD.

FEEL IT ME circles back to what we discussed in chapter 1—the need to sort yourself out and grow yourself up so that you can be immensely present to the journey of parenting. You will do this moment by moment, over and over again. And just when you think you have it figured out, you will fall back into a hole of your own programming and fail once more. That is the process of growth, of figuring out who you are. As adults, we must accept that feeling anxious, angry, or judged about a child's undesirable behaviours—whether that is crying, screaming, tantrums, whining, or sibling aggression—is more about having programs of reaction triggered within us than about our child causing us to feel this way. We must do the work as individuals so that we can do our work as parents. And yes, this work is hard. You will fail repeatedly. That comes with being human.

Even as a psychologist and educator, I still fall prey to my own programs. I still have to struggle to find a way out so I can return to the business of growth for both myself and my children. Please be reassured when you feel like you are failing—we all do. When your child hits you and your first internal response is an angry "How dare you?!" know that this reaction isn't your child's to own. It's yours. But know also that your reaction is normal and understandable. It's also normal for young children to lash out physically. It is part of how they figure it all out. You, the adult, are not meant to hit or shout or otherwise behave like your child. If you find yourself in that place, own it and figure out what is fuelling that feeling of anger. With focus and inner work, you will fail "better" next time. Even if all you can hold onto in the moment is acute awareness, this simple realization will allow you to respond more capably than if you charge in blind when you find yourself feeling angry or otherwise triggered by your child's crying or behaviours. You have power over your response to your child. So why not choose growth? Choosing growth means freedom from old, embedded, habitual reactions that don't serve you or your child, that bring you stress instead of peace. Getting to choose peace, freedom, growth—that is magic.

FEEL IT CHILD is what happens when you have sorted the programs that might be prompting your own discomfort and are able to move past FEEL IT ME. FEEL IT CHILD is where you understand and feel what is happening with and for your child. Let's circle back to your toddler who is losing it at the end of a long trip to the grocery store. They have had enough! They are tired and grocery shopping is so boring! Or perhaps your baby is crying endlessly because something has her feeling out of sorts. That will feel disorienting for a child who isn't old enough to know what her feelings are, let alone old enough to name and share them with you. Or perhaps your daughter just hit her brother. Of course, he took her toy and she isn't old enough yet to understand what sharing is.

BE IT happens when you arrive in your child's emotional space and understand what is happening for them. This will be a seamless transition if you move through FEEL IT ME and FEEL IT CHILD. But I'm going to let you in on a little secret. The truth is that you don't need this book, a psychologist, a parent coach, or anyone else to tell you what to do with your child if you can get what it is to BE IT. If you respond to each individual child's behaviours every time with exactly the same strategy or tactics that have been outlined for them by some well-intentioned expert, you are not BEing in the moment. All crying, tantrums, and acting out looks the same, but it doesn't all come from the same place.

There are plenty of times when I have no idea what I am going to do or say with my children in the moment. But I know that my clear intent is to provide a place for them to lean into while I respond to whatever is going on. Be and then do. Your doing will flow from your being. So get clear about what your BEing is. Imagine the energy. Imagine the feeling. Imagine what it is like to be confident and in the lead. Now manifest that. When you surrender to what is happening in the moment and allow your action to flow from that place, you release your attachment to the "but what do I do" kind of questioning.

This means that I can't tell you specifically what to do in any given moment and still have you come across as a parent who is in charge. If I did tell you what to do, here's what would happen:

that solution might work for you first thing tomorrow morning with your child, but if you were to use that same response in reaction to the same behaviour again at 10 a.m. or 3 p.m. or one of the other fifty-seven times it is going to come up for you on an average day with a toddler in tow, it might well fail. Why? Simple. It wouldn't be coming from a place of BEing. You would be doing without being. Which is why **See It, Feel It, Be It** is where it's at.

Are You Large and In Charge?

It does take time to get the hang of **See It, Feel It, Be It** so that you can be sure to have your large-and-in-charge self operating consistently, especially if you are a new parent or still working through some of your own programming. Here are some signs that will tell you when things are as they should be—and when they are not.

When a child is in the perfect leaning-in position it does not mean that everything is going to be sunshine and roses, that they are going to accept your guidance and see the wisdom in your requests every time. In fact, if that is how a child presented, I would be very concerned! Healthy development is designed to include resistance and upset. As you will see in chapter 5, messiness is the perfect indicator that all is going exactly as it should in the journey of development. However, it is easier to help a child grow when the nurturing hierarchy that nature intended for the parent-child relationship is securely in place. Here are some signs that you have succeeded:

- Your child may have some resistance to activities or requests some of the time, but with gentle and firm guidance they generally acquiesce without a meltdown.
- Your child appears to understand that it is futile to attempt to have the last word or get their own way.

- In times of high stress, big upset, fright, or other moments of emotional activation, your child looks to you as the ultimate source of comfort and guidance.
- Your child checks in with you before setting out to explore something new most of the time.
- When you respond to your upset child they calm relatively quickly most of the time.
- You have a sense of peace in your relationship with your child.

All children will struggle some of the time and push back against your lead position. That struggle is not only normal but necessary to their healthy development. So it is not a concern if this resistance is a regular part of life with your little. This behaviour does become a concern when the child knows no other way to engage with you except to take that lead position. How can you know when a child is taking charge? In the list below are examples of telltale signs. Some children will manifest several of these behaviours, while others will exhibit just one or two, but in large ways. Remember that *all* children will show some of these behaviours occasionally, so the presence of one or more does not necessarily suggest that you have a child who is moving into or stuck in the lead position. Instead, stay alert for a child who appears stuck in a pattern of resistance to you rather than exhibiting smaller and/or more occasional occurrences.

- Your child is unable to accept things from you at face value. You can say the sky is blue and she will argue to the death that it is green.
- Your child may not accept reassurance from you. This can manifest as anxiety—such as an anxious child who refuses to be placated with your gentle murmurs of comfort and fact-telling about the situation at hand.
- Your child will not allow you an original idea; instead, they claim these as their own.

- Your child won't accept food from you. Accepting food from another puts a person in a place of vulnerability. If a child feels they can't count on their parent, they may instinctively refuse food from them.
- Your child will not accept your soothing. This is different from the child who continues to cry because of discomfort or other pain but is still able to receive your comfort.
- Your child is disconcerted by your happiness and looks for ways to call it out or undermine it. For example, they might see your pleasure in telling a joke and then insist that it isn't funny.
- Your child believes you to be a liar about things that matter—for example, when you tell them that you didn't lose their favourite stuffie; it's just in the washing machine. They do not accept your word at face value and insist on checking or being shown that what you say is true.

A parent will know (trust me) that a change in leadership has taken place when a child is stuck in a pattern of being *unable* to lean on the parent and does not see the parent as capable, kind, trustworthy, and competent.

How Your Swagger Gets Disrupted

When a child steps into the lead in the parent-child relationship, this compromises the child's development. Why? Because there is a natural hierarchical ordering to the parent-child relationship that must endure for development to unfold. Like the relationships of teacher and student, boss and employee, guru and follower, without an understood and felt hierarchy the entire experience shifts. The difference between these relationships and the parent-child relationship is that the child's entire life-course is completely affected by a dissolution in the hierarchical nature of the relationship. The child cannot grow as intended if the parent is not in the lead. And, as discussed earlier, a parent cannot be in the lead if they have not fully grown up themselves. There are, however, other forces that may have disrupted the hierarchical nature of the parent-child relationship, and most of them whirl around the practices of raising children. Here are the three forces I believe have the most destructive impact on whether or not a parent truly steps in and takes charge.

The Rise of the "Parenting" Industry

When I was a child my parents did not attend parenting workshops because there weren't any to attend. They didn't read books on parenting, not even Dr. Spock's bestselling tome, *The Common Sense Book of Baby and Child Care.* No shelves at the local bookstore were reserved for parenting books because there were not enough books to fill them. My parents did not attend group discussions about discipline, and they certainly didn't hire parent coaches. If my grandparents were still alive and I were to ask them about "parenting" as a subject that you studied, they would probably be gobsmacked. I am not saying that staying informed and aware as a parent is a terrible thing. I did write this book, after all, and I am one of those psychologists and parent educators who teaches and speaks about parenting in addition to keeping up with the latest research.

However, it is my belief that the "parenting" industry has sprung up from an angst-ridden place. In some ways, the parenting industry has played on the anxiety created by the dissolution of the cultural structures meant to support parents. The frantic nature of modern-day society, the heightened focus on early achievement, and the perceived need to be competitive in our modern world all play into that angst. Parents are surrendering their lead position to so-called experts who purport to know more than they do. Don't get me wrong: Not all of the parenting information available is bad. Knowledge is power, and the wealth of knowledge available today about child development has the potential to change how we understand and grow our children. But parents need to feel empowered by that knowledge rather than submit to it out of bewilderment and angst. We need to seek that knowledge with gusto and swagger rather than from a place of "What if I do it wrong?"

In this sea of parenting knowledge, you can often feel awash in way too much information. Dr. Lapointe says to do it this way. Dr. So-and-So says to do it an entirely different way. Timeouts are good for kids. Timeouts are bad for kids. Groundbreaking research says that playing on digital tablets is educational for children. More groundbreaking research says that playing on tablets is bad for children.

Not only do we have many conflicting points of view on parenting, but those points of view are also right at our fingertips. You only have to do a quick internet search on how to handle a child who won't sleep, or a child who is biting, or a child who is hitting, and suddenly, hours later, you find yourself in a tangled maze of information. Some of it is misleading; much of it is conflicting; some of it amounts to fear-mongering; and, even worse, some of it is downright harmful. As you soak in this often-contradictory information you may start to feel less in the know when it comes to your own child. The constant tidal wave of advice leaves you vulnerable to becoming separated from an intuitive sense of who your child is, what they need, and exactly how you are going to bring that to life. The parenting industry can leave parents bewildered and uncertain. Now how's that for being in charge? My point exactly. You cannot be in charge if you are constantly swimming in a sea of information that leads you to be inconsistent and confused about how to parent. But you also don't need to throw the parenting industry out the window.

In 2017, journalist Leah McLaren wrote an article in which she took on the parenting industry and especially the aspects of it that leave parents feeling like they need to step up their game. Published in one of Canada's leading national papers, the piece was titled "Don't Worry about What the 'Experts' Say: The Kids Are Going to Be All Right."[2] McLaren's opening salvo was to challenge a thesis put forth by well-known psychologist and physician Dr. Leonard Sax. In his 2015 book, ominously titled *The Collapse of Parenting*, Sax posited that parents have lost their way and the kids are now in charge. Books like this tend to lead parents down a rabbit hole of second-guessing. But in her article, McLaren described in detail, and with statistic after statistic, how great kids have it these days and what a good job most parents are doing.

Do I think that there is room for improvement? Sure. When we know better we need to commit to doing better. You don't need to banish Dr. Google forever, but remember to consume the information offered while you occupy the full force of your parenting swagger to keep the parent-child hierarchy intact.

The Misinterpretation of Attachment-Centred Parenting

As someone who is clearly on the side of attachment-centred parenting as a way of raising young children, the fact that I'm raising concerns about it may sound like contradictory, crazy talk. However, it is my belief that the movement has a seedy underbelly. As more parenting educators, psychologists, and other "experts" spread the word about how vital relationship is to the healthy growth and development of our kids, certain messages have landed, but sometimes their meaning gets a little distorted. Society is starting to understand that kids need to be championed and cared for, and that discipline practices like timeouts, consequences, and spanking don't work to foster development but rather interrupt it. We have developed systems (however flawed) of child protection and family law designed to preserve the rights of the child in a divorce and in the foster care system, and to ensure the child's right to their key relationships is preserved so that they have the best possible chance of success.

However, one message of attachment-centred parenting has gone sideways, and that is *the science of relationship* as it pertains to child development. The science of relationship is that a child's existence in the context of a properly functioning parent-child dynamic allows a child's brain to grow as intended. This is the authentic meaning of attachment-centred parenting. However, a surface understanding of attachment-focused parenting can lead to big problems. The surface approach mistakenly dictates that children are meant to be treated with respect *so that they can be happy*.

Consider the parent who works from sun-up to sundown to make sure their child is happy. As a result, that child's existence is only ever a gentle, loving, caring, smooth ride. A parent can twist themselves into a pretzel trying to create such an out-of-reach, unnatural reality. But this isn't what children need. In this scenario, the true-north point of the relational dynamic is spun in a different direction. Making kids happy is not the goal of attachment-centred parenting. Kids who are settled, adaptable (see chapter 5), and feel worthy of love—that is the goal.

Children need a capable caregiver who is kind, loving, *and* in charge. When this is the case, the child can rest. Most important, the child gets the chance to face life's difficulties rather than having a parent erase the moments of adaptation and opportunities to develop resilience (see page 105). This is the scientific truth behind attachment-focused parenting. But this truth runs counter to the unofficial attachment-centred parenting manifesto that suggests parents should not step into their power, especially if it makes a kid unhappy. When a parent does not step into their power there is only one result: an overly permissive parent with porous boundaries, full of nervous energy about messing up, and in the process messing up their kids. A parent who is most definitely not in charge.

The heart of attachment-centred parenting is based on two foundational concepts. The first is that there is a natural hierarchy to the parent-child relationship in which the parent is decidedly in the power position, though from a place of relationship, connection, and compassion. The second is that attachment-focused parenting is not synonymous with an always-all-the-time-no-matter-what happy child. No challenge, no growth. As a parent, you will need to recognize when to allow challenge to present for your child, and when to step in and smooth the road. But understand that even when you are not "fixing" the challenge, you must always be available to understand and support your child.

Another misconception of attachment-centred parenting is that it is often erroneously conflated with the phenomenon of helicopter parenting. Helicopter parenting is a term used to describe a parent who hovers over their child, anxiously attempting to prevent upset, distress, mess, or uncertainty. An attachment-centred parent who is attuned to their child's developmental needs and who is full of swagger will know that struggle is the key to growth, while also knowing when it is appropriate to step in on behalf of the child and support them in finding a way through. This is completely different from the angst-ridden helicopter parent. Yes, as an attachment-centred parent you are meant to really show up and be there for your child, but that appearance is not born of anxiety. Rather, you show up full of confident energy that allows your wisdom to flow, just as it did for me when Chelsea's toppled tiara threatened to ruin the party for her.

Focusing on Peer Orientation

When a child isn't getting along well with others, it is often recommended that they participate in a social skills group—with a bunch of kids who are also struggling with social skill development. Or when a child has a hard time making friends, as one of my boys did in first grade, the go-to solution is to schedule more playdates. But where is the hierarchy in these homogenous groups of children? Where does a child access the closeness of the parent-child or teacher-child or big person–child relationship for rest so they can direct attention to growth and development? Kids are not meant to raise other kids. This is a job for an adult.

Before the education system was formalized, young children were often raised in heterogeneous groups that included adults who educated them according to what they thought they needed to know. Children played and explored and, wouldn't you know, learned a lot. Early in the twentieth century the formalized education system began lumping big masses of same-aged children together in classrooms—a far cry from the multi-age, one-room schoolhouse. But the creation of formal education systems was not based in child development. Rather it was about bolstering economics. The masses needed educating so that individual countries could secure a reasonable, economic position in the global community.

Parents, however, began to absorb the message that they should expose their children to more social interaction with their peers earlier in life; the idea was that by the time the children got to the classroom, they would be "ready" and more likely to be "successful." A hundred or so years later, we throw birthday parties for groups of two-year-olds, thinking that such get-togethers serve their normal development. To me, this kind of thinking is simply weird; from a developmental perspective, kids that age don't even know that each other exist. They still engage in what developmentalists call "parallel play"; they don't play *with* each other, they play beside each other. Children won't begin to understand the back-and-forth of peer interaction until age three or, more likely, four.

Dr. Gordon Neufeld and Dr. Gabor Maté wrote about this phenomenon in their book *Hold Onto Your Kids: Why Parents Need to*

Matter More Than Peers.[3] And what is their aptly communicated thesis? Kids don't need other kids. Kids need their parents and close attachments when it comes to meeting their developmental needs. If a young child looks around at a birthday party for someone to tend to their hurt feelings or another need, and their close attachments are nowhere to be found, who will they turn to? Peers. If this scenario is repeated frequently, the parent will be demoted by default. The parent is no longer in charge because their influential relationship has been replaced by a relationship with a classmate or playmate too often. This is problematic in terms of a child's capacity for emotional rest and healthy development.

The bottom line is that these three disruptors are still tremendously influential in the parenting world. As a parent today, you will need to figure out how to stay in the lead position with your child and prevent these significant forces from undermining that precious relationship hierarchy.

Conquer Your Mountain

What will allow you to maintain your position as a parent who is in charge? Striking a brilliant balance between being firm and being kind. Although I cannot offer you a script for how to be in charge at every moment in your child's life, I can give you a roadmap—one that includes a mountain. And the view from the top is exactly where you want to be: a big person who is large and in charge while also being caring and compassionate—that's solid gold for your growing child.

If you get too attached to being firm, you will tumble down the side of the mountain that has your child experiencing and perceiving you as simply being mean. And when you are seen as mean you are not in charge. Your child will not be able to lean into you because they'll be too busy trying to get away from you and your bullying behaviour. In fact, as your relationship takes hit after hit, your child might develop something called "counterwill,"[4] which may encourage them to become resistant to your leadership and feel inclined to do the opposite of what you have asked. This can lead to your child being large and in charge, rather than you being capably in the lead.

If, however, you are overly attached to being kind, you will tumble down the other side of the mountain—the side that has your child experiencing you as an unreliable, push-over parent. This is illustrative of the seedy underbelly of attachment-centred parenting discussed earlier. Obviously, this doesn't serve your child or the relationship between you. In this state, when your child tries to lean into you, they will find you incapable of the support and guidance they need because you are wishy-washy about the boundaries. Again, this means that they will be catapulted into the lead position and unable to endure the uncertainty of not having a guide on this massive journey called life.

My experience with families—whether two-parent in one household or across two households—is that one parent becomes the almighty Mr. or Mrs. Firm while the other parent becomes the pandering Mr. or Mrs. Kind. Mr. or Mrs. Firm staunchly defends their position, saying they don't have a choice but to be this way because the other parent is incapable of setting boundaries and meaning what they say. And Mr. or Mrs. Kind similarly defends their position, saying they have to be this way because the other parent is so mean and reactive all the time. The truth is that they are both wrong. Both need to summon the energy and insight to get themselves right back up to the peak of that mountain so they can really be what their child needs. And remember, it only takes one. If you find that you are co-parenting with someone unable to make that mountainous ascent, take heart: even by making the ascent on your own, you are light years ahead for the well-being of your child.

The bottom line is that being in charge really means BEing the big person. In the words of Wayne Dyer, "You are a human being rather than a human doing."[5] If you worry endlessly about how you are supposed to do this, and exactly what it is that your child needs, and what will happen if you mess it up, then you have lost the plot. Go back inside. Where did things go off track? What part of your child self is reacting right now? What might you do to reassure/parent your child self so that your adult self is fully present and able to step in as needed for the child outside that you are now raising? What is the story you are telling yourself that maybe needs some reworking so that you can be present again?

Find Your Village

The reality of being a parent, especially to a baby or toddler or preschooler who is utterly dependent upon you, can be incredibly challenging. You are on 24/7. Nobody else can be you and know your child as intimately as you do. And, on top of this, you are likely in the most profound period of growth and development that you have experienced to this point in your adult life. It is extremely difficult to be a constant source of steady presence and to support your growing child when you feel that your own needs for support are going unmet. You are meant to have that support as a parent. We were never meant to go this alone. You should have a community of people supporting you through this journey. Who do you lean into? Parenting educator and author Ann Douglas wrote about this in *Happy Parents, Happy Kids*, in which she shines a light on how a community can come together in support of parents and children.[6]

Find your support so you can be supportive. But if support is lacking, create it for yourself, whether through friends, parent groups, or local child development centres and programs. Be aware that one village usually can't support you fully. In my own life, I turn to different support villages: my family, my local community, and my personal development/parenting colleagues. My family lives far away, but when I am feeling overwhelmed and want to lean in and be held, there is no one like my mom. When I am speaking at an evening workshop and my dogs need walking and my kids need dinner, my community is there for me. When I am stuck in a story, my personal development village guides me to the cause of my stressful thinking.

As you search for support, try not to get too caught up in the story that tells you "this parenting gig is hard!" You might read that statement and think, "No way—that's not a story! It really is hard! That is an undeniable truth!" Trust me—I hear you. And yet, it *is* a story.

I recall listening to Eckhart Tolle talk about how rainy and cloudy it is for eight months of the year in my hometown of Vancouver, Canada. He said how you experience this is a direct reflection of the story you have made up about it. When you believe that rain and clouds are dreary and depressing, that leads you down one experiential path. When you believe that rain and clouds are refreshing and cleansing, it leads you down another path. The invitation I make here to you is to quiet the stories of the mind and sit within the present moment so that you can experience what is rather than what you *think is*.

When I am consumed by fearful thoughts that are distracting me from the present I recall this mantra:

> All there is
> is this moment
> and this moment is perfect.

So, what if there are dark clouds and rain is falling from the sky. Sit with that. And nothing more. Then, as you *choose* the narrative you will weave around this, choose one that works for you. Here's how that works in a parenting context: Your child is crying. Now, you may be thinking, "This kid is so needy! Will they ever stop crying? If this is my life for the next six months, I will die!" That is one story. But there's another way you could think about this: "My child is crying and I am the all-powerful, present adult, so it does not matter if my child settles or not. What matters is that I am here for them." That is a completely different story. The experience that will flow from the story is based on the narrative you weave around it. As you walk your path of being a parent, think about what story you will *choose*—for it is a choice. You have free will in this. If you don't like your story then choose another one. And keep choosing it. Think thoughts that feed your preferred story. Speak "truths" that feed your preferred story. And keep choosing. Thought after thought.

In her book *Loving What Is*, Byron Katie wrote that you grow yourself up by accepting what is. You can argue with reality... and you will lose 100 percent of the time. This argument will create stress and upset in your life. But everything shifts and changes when you understand that nothing happens *to you*; rather, everything happens *for you*. Thinking in this way allows you to feel gratitude for situations that might otherwise be frustrating. You can be grateful for your crying baby, your misbehaving toddler, your pesky preschooler, secure in the knowledge that they are giving you the greatest gift—the chance to continue to grow yourself. The acceptance of this knowledge profoundly changes how you step into your in-charge role as a parent. Not *give in* but *step in*. You step in and step up and be for your child from a present, accepting, surrendered place. And from that place, you will do and be exactly what your child needs.

When you care for a tiny human you are witnessing huge potential for growth and development. What a wonderful opportunity to find yourself capably in charge. Even if you are tired, overwhelmed, or questioning whether you have the mental energy to get the job done, know that it is worth all the soul-revealing effort to climb that mountain. Be big. Invite your child to lean in. Create huge invitation for this. Script a story that works for you and feed that narrative in the full wisdom that it is a choice you make every moment of every day. Now is the time.

See It, Feel It, Be It.

5

BIG, BEAUTIFUL MESS

Y OUR KID IS having a meltdown for the twelfth time today and you are at the end of your rope. Does it have to be this hard, this loud, this persistent? What if I told you that your child's meltdown is a sign that things are going well? What if you understood that your child *needs* to lose it—many times over—so that his brain will grow, and so that he'll become an adult capable of impulse control and empathy, of making solid choices in difficult situations, and with the ability to move through his emotions with ease and power. That is how it's *supposed* to work during a child's first three or four years of life. When your child struggles and is invited to experience that struggle in the presence of your loving and safe compassion, you turn your child's meltdown into a parenting win. That's right— toddler tantrums for the win.

Unfortunately, Western culture doesn't always look favourably upon the louder, messier parts of being a little one. Somehow we've conflated parental competence with child development and come up with knee-jerk judgments about a child's behaviours and, by default, the ways in which those behaviours reflect on the parents. Say there's a child losing it in the grocery store because his request for a treat has been met with a "no." How many of the strangers passing by may be thinking, "That parent needs to set firmer limits more often," or "Clearly the message about the greedy gimmees hasn't gotten through to that one yet," or "What a spoiled little nag"? Reactions such as these implicitly assign a label of "good" or "bad" to the child and the parent. You are a good child if you are submissive and agreeable. You are a good parent if you have a child who is submissive and agreeable. Have a child who loses it? Obviously, you are a bad parent. And what about the child who loses it? Obviously, he is a bad child. Even if people don't give voice to such judgments, they lurk beneath the surface—a lingering bias of generations past when children were thought to be blank slates[1] or evil beings needing to be shown the light.

When you are feeling uncertain or overwhelmed in a challenging parenting situation, you are more vulnerable to being governed by your own subconscious programming. This makes it easier for you to fall into the trap of parenting to placate cultural biases rather than serving the true needs of your child's development. Depending on what your programming is, your need to make sure you do it all perfectly or to avoid conflict can turn your parenting upside down.

When my youngest son struggled within the traditional classroom setting at school, I intuitively understood that he needed to be moved. But I questioned myself. Was I doing too much to smooth his pathway? Was I reading too much into his experiences, and would my training work against me? Would I, the psychologist, do this wrong? I scheduled meetings, paid for assessments, gave him mental health days, and then pushed him into continued attendance in the traditional school setting. I cried oceans of tears until, five years later, I woke up one morning and decided I was done with the angst. I registered my son in another school that day.

Of course, the process of putting my intuition into action was layered and complicated. It's likely my son stayed too long in his old school because I played into both my programming and the programming of his father. You too may end up catering to your programs and the programs of other adults around you instead of tending to your child's unique, wonderful, naturally existing needs. Our instinctual tendency to cater first to our interior programs, and not to the needs of our child, makes it important for parents to be deeply aware of what is operating beneath the surface in their journey through life. Creating this awareness will help to prevent the inadvertent sabotaging of a child's development to serve your own unmet needs.

Nothing about natural, normal, healthy child development is triggering or upsetting. Bear that in mind if you are feeling fired up by what you observe in your child. This is a call for you to explore why you are reacting the way you are. You will discover that the answer is never going to be "My child is making me react this way." It will always be your "inner child" that has set the reaction in motion. As discussed in chapter 1, it is the story you tell yourself about what you are observing in your child's development that sets you off. That story is deeply influenced by the bias of your perceptions, which were created when your mind was formed during your childhood. This story, then, is not an accurate reflection of your current reality—unless you believe it to be or make it so.

No Challenge, No Growth

Children struggle, meltdown, and have tantrums because they *must*—not because they are bad or manipulating you but because they need to struggle to grow. When a child's brain fires in response to challenging circumstances and the brain is calmed through your caregiving, this allows for the development of the pathways that govern the capacity for impulse control in the prefrontal cortex. But this happens only over time and through many thousands of repetitions. This neural activity also allows for the shaping of pathways in the downstairs brain so that children learn to work through big emotions and settle themselves. The repetition of this process is neuroplasticity in action, and it must happen this way so that the necessary pathways are etched into the evolving architecture of the developing brain. As those pathways take hold, your child will develop impulse control, empathy, the capacity to make good choices in difficult situations, and the ability to move through emotions with ease and power.

But when you are raising a child in a culture soaked in the belief that agreeableness is a desirable trait, you may find yourself acting in a way that serves the judgmental gaze of that culture instead of your child's needs. You may blame your three-year-old for having a tantrum in reaction to something that didn't go their way, or your two-year-old for not sharing (even though sharing is still an alien concept for them developmentally). You angrily shush your crying child, concerned that his wails are disturbing people around you. Parents may act without knowing what they are doing or why, simply to be looked upon as a good parent. I have heard about parents who were advised to bite their two-year-old in response to the child's bites to shame them and "teach them a lesson." Why? So they can have a "good" child who doesn't bite, and so they, in turn, can be seen as a "good" parent.

To parent right from the start means knowing and accepting that children must struggle in order for their brains to grow. A smooth ride with no upset, no invitation for strife, no need to accept that which cannot be does not produce growth. It produces stagnation. When your child cries, has tantrums, wakes up constantly, or otherwise struggles to find themselves in a calm, neurologically regulated state, and you provide comfort and surround them with compassion so that they feel seen and heard, their brain grows. But if you hurry-scurry around your child to kick away the obstacles, smooth the bumps, move the boundaries you've established, and change all the things that upset them, you rob them of that opportunity. You erase growth in the name of comfort, convenience, and ease. What is comfortable, convenient, and easy is not always what is good. And when it comes to your child's healthy development, it has to get messy in order to be beautiful. No challenge, no growth. What a big, beautiful mess!

And here's something amazing to consider: as you allow the mess to exist, you will slowly and surely see that it untangles itself. How? The untangling happens when you stay steady in your provision of compassion and comfort. Not perfect, but steady. How does a child's brain figure out what it is to sleep through the night? Through you calming them back to sleep with your safe and comforting presence. How does a child's brain figure out what to do when they flip out because a toy cannot be had? Through you calming them to a place of acceptance and showing them how this goes, how this feels, how this lands. How does a child's brain sort out what it is to manage impulses and not strike out in anger, push, shove, or steal that which is wanted right now? When you demonstrate what that looks like with heaps—no, mountains—of understanding and compassion alongside your firm, boundary-setting presence.

So, if challenge is good for your child's growth, should you strive to create opportunities for challenge in their daily life? No. The normal ups and downs of life will offer enough challenges without well-intended, overzealous intervention. Trust this resolutely.

Indeed, if you inject extra challenge in your child's world you may create a reality that is too overwhelming for your child to cope with. And when a child becomes overwhelmed by a world that is simply too much for them they don't get stronger—they reach a breaking point. Neurologically speaking, that breaking point occurs when the brain is too flooded to cope. If this happens too intensely and/or too often, the result is a child who is perpetually dysregulated. You can see this in a child with the enduring inability to be soothed or calmed, or even a child who appears to be numb to it all, because to sit in continual upset is too difficult and too challenging. Trust instead that your child's life will come with enough challenge of its own. Your job is to support them in sitting in the discomfort of that challenge so that growth can occur.

Dandelion or Orchid?

Part of what influences the intensity of the big, beautiful mess that defines healthy child development will be determined by what makes your child their own amazing person. Every child is born wired a little differently, a situation that results in each of them having a unique temperament. As it turns out, temperament will play a central role in the degree to which your child must rail against the things in his life that aren't working for him before he is developmentally and emotionally able to come into a space of adaptation and find another way through the upset. No matter what your child's temperament is, though, the brain's capacity for neuroplasticity will help them manoeuvre capably through the big, beautiful mess and come out the other side a well-adjusted and settled human. Remember, neurons that fire together wire together (see page 64), so staying steady in your provision of external regulation is essential regardless of your child's temperament.

The most helpful description of temperament I've ever come across is in a 2005 article written by human development specialists W. Thomas Boyce and Bruce J. Ellis.[2] The authors borrowed two Swedish words to explain opposite ends of the human temperament continuum: *orkidebarn*, which translates to "orchid child," and *maskrosbarn*, which translates to "dandelion child."

The dandelion is known for surviving in the most challenging of circumstances. Not enough water? No problem. Too hot? No problem. Not enough nutrients? Also no problem. Not only will the dandelion survive in the face of challenging circumstances, but it can even thrive. The dandelion child is resilient. The dandelion child goes with the flow. The dandelion child can weather the storms of a less than optimal home environment, or an upsetting or traumatic event, or inconsistent, unreliable parenting, and they will likely be fine, or even better than fine.

Not so the orchid. If you have ever tried to grow an orchid you will know that it takes patience, wisdom, and presence to help it thrive. Too much or too little sunlight and the plant dies. Too much or too little water and the plant dies. Too hot or too cold and the plant dies. The orchid child is the same. This is the child who requires "just right" conditions to thrive. When that happens, the outcome is spectacular. But when it doesn't happen, the outcome may be devastating. The orchid child is immensely sensitive to parenting approaches. Sensitive kids may appear messier for longer, but not because they are developmentally delayed. A child who is born highly sensitive will need more time for their brain to mature before self-regulation becomes an available skill set. Patience will win the day.

Though some children will be straight-up orchid or straight-up dandelion in their temperament, most children exist somewhere on the spectrum between these two poles. These children may display orchid-esque tendencies in certain aspects of their temperament but be more dandelion-esque in others. For example, a child may be intensely sensitive to the emotions of others, resulting in heightened reactivity, but may not be fussy at all about the food he gets to eat, the clothes he has to wear, or the fact that it's time to stop playing and settle in for a nap.

In their article, Boyce and Ellis made a case for a genetic link to the orchid-dandelion presentation in a child, and subsequent research has confirmed that there is indeed a genetic transmission of these temperament traits. But however the orchid-dandelion aspects manifest in your child, it is misleading to account for them solely based on genetics. Genes may express themselves differentially based on experience. As revealed in chapter 1, the study of epigenetics has allowed scientists to understand that certain genetic factors can be heightened or suppressed based on the environment around a child, especially at key periods in their development, such as the first few years of life.

For example, if a child is born to an anxious, intense parent, the orchid genetic expression may be amplified so that the child can "adapt" to that particular child-parent dynamic by becoming hypervigilant. The expression of the orchid tendency may similarly be heightened if a child is born into a chaotic home environment. In that case, the child becomes even more sensitive so that they are appropriately prepared for the next unpredictable event, which means they are always in a state of stress. A dandelion child may also be influenced in the same way, and may end up similarly existing in a perpetual state of stress if their environment primes them for that. The orchid child is already sensitive, so they may be more vulnerable or predisposed to being highly influenced by their environment compared to the dandelion child, who may perhaps tolerate more before being tipped over into a state of perpetual stress.

The dandelion child is more often than not less sensitive to the environment around them and to their internal state. So even an anxious or intense parent-child relationship may not have as much of an impact on them. However, this is not to say that anything goes for the dandelion child. All children have a limit of what they can tolerate. The orchid child? You might as well be standing on your head juggling flaming swords while trying to pull the perfect espresso shot (to sustain your exhausted self, obviously); it *still* won't be enough to dial down the sensitivity. No matter how much comfort you offer, they will still need to have a big reaction. Dandelion babes will react too, but that reaction doesn't need to be as massive, and they tend to settle down quickly.

Most problematic for the orchid babe is that the more they swim around in the sensitivity swamp, the more their brains become good at being dysregulated. And the more time a child spends dysregulated without being calmed by their parent, the greater the likelihood of challenges with sleeping, stress management, and overall mental health down the road.

Happily, if parents respond consistently with a comforting presence to the bids put out by the ultrasensitive orchid babe, the child's exquisitely fired-up brain is more likely to become exquisitely adept at calming. Over the coming years (patience, please!), the orchid child will grow into a well-adjusted adult. One who is a big feeler. One who probably adjusts certain things in his environment to suit his constitution. One who does amazing things with the amazing brain their parents helped grow. And what of the dandelion child? Under conditions optimal for healthy growth and development—namely the presence of an attuned caregiver who is readily available for support and co-regulation—that child will go on to be equally amazing. While dandelion kiddos are less sensitive than their orchid counterparts, they still have big needs that require the steady presence of a big person who is full of swagger.

Development and Individuation

Around the end of the first year of life, alongside the neurological growth that is behind a child's burgeoning capacity for self-soothing, the process of individuation—how your child will emerge into their own person—also begins. But remember that the capacity for impulse control, making good choices, and regulating emotions is not yet within reach for your child. And still, they are striding confidently along his own developmental path. However, children start this process of becoming their own person without any internal capacity for policing themselves. Boom! Welcome to the start of what many refer to as the "Terrible Twos."

This unfortunate moniker comes from the juxtaposition of an emerging sense of self with an inability to control that emerging self. There is nothing at all problematic about either of these realities, or the big, loud, beautiful mess of their side-by-side existence. And yet, this very same mess can be thought of as inconvenient—*if* we choose to tell ourselves that story. We may refer to this stage of a child's development as "terrible" when it is, in fact, remarkable! Do you really want to grow a submissive, compliant, numb human being? Of course not. So get ready to welcome the beautiful mess of toddlerhood. Terrible Twos? No. *Terrific* Twos!

As individuation progresses, the toddler begins to understand that he stands separate from his parent. Not until somewhere around a child's second birthday does he even realize that you and he are not the same person. In his mind, *he is you*. Over the next two to three years, and by around the age of five, the child arrives at the understanding that he is his own person: that rather than *being his parent*, he is what is *created by his parent*. This understanding grows until somewhere around the start of adolescence, when the next big step in the process of individuation occurs, and is accompanied by the almost ubiquitous rites of passage that parents of adolescents fretfully anticipate. But even in the face of young adulthood, you don't just sit back and watch the transition happen. As you show your teen the way through those developmentally typical (and occasionally challenging) behaviours, he takes another big step toward becoming his own person. Here, he recognizes that he is what is *created by his parent and by himself*. And then finally, somewhere in early adulthood, he will step fully into realizing that he is what he himself creates. *He is himself*. He has arrived.

Sounds simple, right? If only. As I map out neurodevelopment alongside the process of individuation, you'll begin to understand what happens at each stage, how you can help make it happen, and why it's all meant to be loud, and colourful, and messy.

Infancy to Two Years

The overall process of individuation starts at birth with a baby who has no concept of the distinction between where she ends and where you begin. The baby believes she and her parent are one and the same. She makes sense of your existence and her own and the dance of your relationship by *being with* you. She absorbs your touch, your taste, your smell, your sound, your rhythm. She absorbs you to the extent that the boundary between the two of you is non-existent. When your baby is born, she does not have the capacity to deal with upset on her own. She needs you to help her find her way back to calm. Her brain literally merges with yours and absorbs all of its regulatory capacity via the relational brain bridge (see page 64) you have created by caring for her in an attuned way. As you do this, her brain and body will begin to figure out the early stages of self-soothing from the experience of being soothed.

Throughout this process it is important that a baby has their key caregivers in close physical proximity and readily available so that all of their needs can be adeptly addressed. As your babe becomes a toddler and starts to establish her own sense of self, she still does not have the neurodevelopmental capacity to manage much as far as self-regulation is concerned. What, then, can a parent expect from a baby or a toddler who is contending with a limitation, a disappointment, or any other situation that is not going her way? The only response available to the toddler is to erupt. That is why parents so closely identify toddlerhood with tantrums and all things difficult. And yet, if your toddler does not experience these eruptions relatively frequently during this period, she will not successfully emerge into her own self.

For toddlers, there is no way around the meltdown. No challenge, no growth. You don't need to make it better. You *do* need to walk alongside your child while her meltdown is occurring. You need to provide a big invitation for it to exist and lots of compassion as it plays out. During this stage, your child should not be labelled "bad" or made to feel wrong for being developmentally unable to sidestep her meltdowns. Your child will need lots of support to navigate the big feelings of her little world. Check out the second half of this book, particularly chapters 8 and 10, for some additional ideas about how to do this.[3]

Three to Five Years

During these years of your child's life, the process of individuation is in full swing and brain development is motoring along. Your child will continue to show signs of wanting to be his own person, such as insisting on doing things for himself, refusing your direction or advice, and so on. However, unlike in the earlier stages of his life—when the only way of coping with a situation that was not going his way was to have a big meltdown—he now has some emerging capacity for acceptance. This is because your compassionate, caring, and empathic responses have started to add up both neurologically (in terms of his brain development) and emotionally (in terms of development of self). Your actions have created an additional option for your child to draw on when challenged. This doesn't mean that emotional eruptions and meltdowns will cease entirely. However, it does mean that your child will begin to move to a place of acceptance more readily and frequently, even if this outcome is still preceded by some tears and upset.

Resilience is a concept we hear about frequently these days. The ability to be resilient begins with the capacity for acceptance.

Acceptance doesn't necessarily mean you are happy with the out-come, but it does mean that you've come to terms with it. This may seem a subtle nuance to add to your child's slate of responses, but it is a very important one developmentally. When your child rages at what is happening in his world but then moves through to acceptance, usually by way of a big bout of sadness, it is a huge step forward in untangling the big, beautiful mess of the early years. The melting of rage into tears is what Dr. Gordon Neufeld calls moving from "mad to sad."

You will need to find the patience and courage to let your little one's emotions run their course while staying steady in the provi-sion of compassion and boundaries. The moment will pass and the transformation will occur naturally, over time, with a lot of repetition. Imagine that your child is screaming in the café you've just entered (oh-so-ready for a cup of coffee!). Everyone is staring or glaring. Your heart is racing and your face is reddening by the second. You may feel surges of shame, embarrassment, desperation, guilt, and even anger. But instead of allowing those feelings to direct your actions, place them aside to be looked at later. Tune into your developing child and his world, his needs. And as you hold him through his yelly-shouties, the wave breaks and his tantrum melts into sobbing, and from there to acceptance and settling. Growth has just happened.

The trick here is to understand that learning how to move from mad to sad does not happen with logic, and it is not a skill that can be taught. It must be experienced. You can't talk a child into accep-tance. Instead, it is the experience of emotional vulnerability that eases the child, and indeed any human being, into the experience of acceptance. This experience is created when you provide space and room for all the upset that precedes the acceptance to take place—space and room that is infused with empathy and understanding so that your child's emotional vulnerability is not threatened.

When a child can remain emotionally open, not fearing shaming or shut-down by his special big people, then the emotions necessary for acceptance will be engaged and the child will move through those emotions to arrive at a place of adapting. When the child is reprimanded for his reactions, he experiences this as shame, and his vulnerability is shut down. In the wise words of Brené Brown, "We live in a world where most people believe that shame is a good tool for keeping people in line. Not only is this wrong, but it's dangerous. Shame is highly correlated with addiction, violence, aggression, depression, eating disorders and bullying. Researchers don't find shame correlated with positive outcomes at all. There are no data to support that shame is a compass for good behavior. In fact, shame is much more likely to be the cause of destructive and hurtful behaviors than it is to be the solution."[4]

So better out than in. If a child gets to experience safe containment of the upset—with boundaries held firmly and compassion flowing freely—emotions move along, vulnerability remains alive, and growth occurs. If the child is shut down or shamed, stagnation will be the result and repercussions will follow. The process of developing the capacity to react, move through this reaction, and ultimately accept the situation is often messy, but always beautiful. And until more time has passed and further development has occurred, this perfect, natural mess is all that is available to your child.

Early Childhood: Five-plus Years

Once you have primed your child for the neurological and emotional capacity for acceptance, the fruits of your labour will become more evident. At this stage your child has the burgeoning capacity to shine with her own incredible, inborn capacity for resilience when the going gets tough. You will have spent the first five years or so of her life allowing her to feel all of her big feelings, to move through the big feelings of reactivity to the big feelings of sad acceptance. Time to add another layer—a layer that will help your child to become capable of regulating her own emotions in the face of conflict, upset, or the need to make a decision. Rather than stopping at the acceptance stage, your child will now be able to move through to some level of self-directed problem-solving and decision-making. But only if the emotional atmosphere is relatively cool. Even though your child is older now, she is not yet fully mature. As soon as the emotional atmosphere becomes heightened—like when she *really* wants that toy or *really* wants an ice cream—and especially when her coping reserves are low because she's tired or hungry or overwhelmed, your child's emerging ability to hang onto control of the situation will waver, and the meltdown, hit, shout, or push will invariably sneak out.

Your child's prefrontal cortex now has the capacity to consider options, even if a scenario is emotionally charged. This leads to self-control in certain situations—such as deciding to share rather than hoarding or stealing a toy from a sibling or peer, or deciding to do what was asked of her rather than charging headfirst into a meltdown. But she won't be able to deliver every single time. Again, this process will take many repeated occurrences and a lot of practice before it permanently sinks in. But sink in it will—with your steadfast, gentle presence leading the way.

THE KEY FOR parents throughout the untangling of the big, beautiful mess of childhood is the creation of a soft invitation, activating that mantra of See It, Feel it, Be It (see page 83). As a parent, your challenge is to take stock of what is happening with your child and stay present in the moment, to be your biggest best self, to feel fully for your child, and then, with that energy of BEing that is fully in charge and completely engaged in the most empathic way, to create space for events and feelings to play out. Even if you cannot see tangible evidence in the moment, know that you are doing exactly what your child needs.

And now, with a thorough understanding of the foundational concepts of parenting right from the start, we are ready to transition to the next part of this book, where I will apply all that you have learned to specific situations, such as aggression, sleep challenges, feeding difficulties, and sibling upsets. With the complete understanding of how important it is to grow yourself so you are fully available to the growing of your child, the full acceptance of relationship as the primary ingredient for healthy child development, and the knowledge that relationship grows brains and allows for development to take place, you are ready to get down to the art of BEing.

THE PLAY CHALLENGE

There is nothing like entering your child's play world to experience the joy of connection. This one act will do amazing things for priming resilience in and developing your relationship with your growing child. So here is a challenge I issue to all my client families, and one I invite you to take up as well:

Play with your child every day for fifteen minutes.

This is a specific kind of playtime in which *all your attention* is focused on child-directed play. Watch your child's face and body language, and look for other cues that will help you be a part of their inner world for these precious fifteen minutes every day. This commitment of connected time allows your child to feel an enormous sense of being seen and heard.

This, in turn, has a tremendously positive impact on the parent-child relationship, and subsequently, a significant buffering effect on later mental health and well-being.[5] If all parents were aware of the importance of playing with their children in this way, we might offset some of the challenges that can come later for our adolescents, such as anxiety and depression.

Dr. Vanessa's
Parenting Principles

OVER THE YEARS, I have developed a list of twelve parenting principles that will help you parent right from the start. Approaching your parenting role intentionally with key principles in mind allows you to stay the course, and when you struggle, helps you to find your way back with perhaps a little more ease.

1. No challenge, no growth
Embrace the mess of life because that is where growth blossoms. Here is where your child's ability to adapt is fostered and resilience is championed. When your children do not experience the challenges of life they cannot grow. Help them navigate challenge with swagger and compassion.

2. Neurons that fire together, wire together
What you do on the outside grows your child on the inside. A young child's brain is designed to soak up environment. You can nurture neural wiring through your caregiving relationship with your children, especially when it comes to helping them develop self-regulation. That's neuroplasticity at work!

3. Grow you, grow them

No one triggers us like our children can. When we explore the origins of these triggers, we discover that often it is the un-grown parts of ourselves from our childhood that are at issue rather than our children's behaviour. Grow you so you can grow them.

4. Swagger is all

Step in to your swagger as the big person on whom your child depends. This is less about "doing" and more about "being." The energy that flows between you and your child must be full of unquestioning competence so you can fulfill your natural role as your child's true north.

5. Relationship is the bottom line

Everything about how humans tick comes down to relationship, which makes it the most crucial need of a developing child. Embrace the relationship with your child. Do nothing, say nothing, be nothing that does not champion relationship as the bottom line.

6. You are enough

Nobody is the expert on a child in the way that the parent is. Your gut, your intuition, your sense of your child's being are unlike anything anybody else can lay claim to. Your child needs you to own this deep knowledge and know, without question, that you are enough.

7. Seek joy

Nurture joy by infusing your parenting journey with gratitude, humour, fun, and playfulness. This is the stuff that makes a child's—and an adult's—world go round. When you are truly present, you will find that being a compassionate witness to your child's growth is an incredibly joyful experience.

8. Find your village

You were never meant to parent alone. We are meant to thrive in villages. Our ancestors lived a rich communal existence and raised their children amid its hustle and bustle and support; today, parents do the same work in relative isolation. It falls upon us to create a community in which to raise our young. Find yours.

9. Foster dependence

Dependence is the natural state of the child. Encourage your child to lean into the caring provision of their capable, empathetic big people. Through leaning in, a child summons the energy for growth. For your child, the true gift of this deep dependence is eventual emergence into the best, independent version of themselves.

10. Know where to set the bar

Set the behaviour bar where your child can reach it. Too high and a child experiences constant failure. Too low and they never experience the joy of conquering life. Both errors force a child to reject your lead. Educate yourself about child development, temperament, and attachment so you can set the bar in the perfect place.

11. Choose stories that feed love

Everything you perceive, including what it is to be a parent and how your child behaves, is a story. Consider deeply what perspective brings you peace, compassion, joy, and gratitude. Actively choose the stories that feed love rather than fear, and view your child through that lens.

12. Slow down

Never rush childhood! Honour the inherent timeline of growth embedded inside your unique child. Development should never be hurried for the sake of convenience or competition. Rushed development may create a desired outcome initially but this result often has no staying power and creates havoc downstream.

PART
TWO

6

SLEEPING

M Y TWO BOYS, now aged twelve and fifteen years, cannot seem to get enough sleep. They've become expert sleepers, and would sleep a solid twelve hours a night plus a nap after school if it were possible. And yet, neither one of them slept through the night without waking at least once until they were eighteen months old. As small babes, both of them would wake several times a night. As toddlers, they liked to start the day between five and six in the morning. One of them slept with me from the age of three until he was six. During the early years of my boys' lives, I received much advice about their sleep patterns, most of which was unsolicited. The overriding beliefs seemed to be that how and when my babes were sleeping needed to be sorted out, their schedules weren't "normal," and that this could spell disaster for healthy sleep habits down the road. I fell prey to some of this advice briefly. Most of it I ignored, choosing instead to follow my intuition, and today, here we are: two expert sleepers in the house.

Even though my boys are now very adept at the art of sleeping, it wasn't really quite as simple as just ignoring all of that unsolicited advice and doing it my own way. In fact, the path through those early days was not simple or easy at all. When my first son was born, I had no idea what it would mean to sleep for no more than two consecutive hours—I was exhausted. Finally, at the age of six weeks, he slept through his first four-hour stretch. I felt like a new woman thanks to those two wonderful, extra hours of sleep. Not long afterwards, though, the whispers began: "He's eight weeks old and he hasn't slept through the night yet?" "You know you will have to teach him how to sleep sooner or later." "He's going to have to figure out how to do a lot of things he doesn't like, so you might as well get started on sleep training now." Sound familiar?

I am often asked what I think about sleep training. Isn't it better for babies to sleep so parents can be their best selves? Here is my bold answer—one that I offer to you based on the science of child development: it depends. It depends on your baby, on you and your temperament, and on extenuating circumstances. It is only when a parent understands how a baby's brain functions and grows that they are able to make sense of the individual and complex circumstances that influence how a baby sleeps, and figure out how to help that process in a healthy way.

Sleep Training is for Adults

You've probably figured out that the traditional version of sleep training has no place in science-based, heart-centred parenting. Any parenting strategy that involves denying your child access to you is, in my view, a non-starter (see pages 30 and 222). Strategies that force the facade of a sleep behaviour in a child simply so that life is more convenient for the adult will not help your child grow up in the best way. You need to focus on what works for your child. So I invite you to dig deep, to think about what your child needs, to script a story that will empower and settle you, and to make decisions that flow from that place instead of from a place of exhaustion, hurry, and frustration. As you consider what this will look and feel like for you and your child, I have a new definition of sleep training to offer you:

Let us redefine sleep training as *changing adult behaviours around child sleep* rather than changing what the child is or does.

Given the current science in child development, we must acknowledge that sleep training is an adult-focused intervention that calibrates the conditions around a child's sleeping patterns. But the usual approaches to sleep training have it backwards in trying to change the child; instead, it is adults who must adjust to make the conditions ideal for the child. No forced separations. No imposed intervals of crying. Instead, redirect your energy and get attuned to your child's needs so that their regulatory system can grow and their emotional needs are met.

Tell Yourself a Happy Bedtime Story

One of the first and most important conditions a parent can adjust is the story they tell themselves about their baby's sleep patterns. If you are stuck in a loop of feeling upset about your baby's sleep, explore this by investigating where that story of upset is coming from. Do you think your baby's sleep patterns are in some way "wrong"? Do you worry about being judged by your spouse, your in-laws, your physician, or your friends? Has a lack of sleep resulted in you telling yourself a big tale of how awful being a parent is? Answer these questions, and then ask how those stories have created stress in you, and perhaps in your baby as well. What if you changed your story? What if you told yourself a different one—one that would allow you, and your baby, to rest easy?

Here's the good news: you can change your story *right now*. You can feed a story of gratitude and empowerment and abundance and love rather than a story of fear and failure and hardship. If you want peace more than chaos, why not decide on a story that you love? One with a happy ending—the kind of happy ending you get to live every day or, in this case, every night. Your story can be that you know your babe will one day sleep through the night—this too shall pass. Determine that you will enjoy the nighttime visits. Think about the day when your baby will be an adolescent and all they'll want to do is sleep—and all you'll want is for them to get out of bed! Feed yourself a story of hope that tomorrow will be better than today, and if it isn't, the next day will be. Better sleep for your baby starts with a better story about your baby's sleep.

Know that while you are busy adjusting your story to positively suit your child's needs, there is also a place for your needs. However, because you are the adult and can manage disruption to your routines so much better than your little one, it is incumbent on you to move toward what works for your child rather than getting stuck on what works for you. Make sure your child gets what she needs so that you don't end up spending unnecessary time fixing a sleep plan that went sideways, and so that she has the best possible shot at healthy development.

If you have a physical or mental health condition that could affect your ability to meet your child's needs around sleep, rely on your supporters to provide the respite you need. My experience is that once stories are dissected and what is adjustable around sleep for your child is adjusted, few people are left feeling as if they are meeting their child's needs at the absolute expense of their own. Even if you are in that group, know that it's okay to ask for help: you are the best parent you can be when you take care of yourself so that you can be otherwise available to your child.

As for what the world says? Never mind that. Let's go with what science says and what our hearts demand. If your baby cries, go to them. And don't feel bad about it for even one second. Go to them every single time.

However, as discussed earlier (see page 57), there is one instance when you should definitely not go to your baby: when you are becoming so overwhelmed and so undone yourself that you might reactively do something that would cause harm. Shaken baby syndrome is a traumatic brain injury that occurs most typically when exhausted and depleted parents shake their baby out of anger and frustration. Babies can die as a result of being shaken, or they may live with permanently impaired brain (and emotional) function. If you find yourself in that kind of state, do not attend to your baby. Make sure they are physically safe, by placing them in a crib or another place that is safe for a baby, and walk away. Take some breaths. Settle yourself. Get help from another caregiver if one is available. Go back to your baby only when you are certain you can trust yourself to minimize your own frustrations to care for your little one.

Adjust for Temperament

It is important to keep the orchid-dandelion temperament distinction (see chapter 5) in mind when making decisions about how to support your baby through sleep. You will want to calibrate and adjust such decisions to the specific needs of your baby and not to some canned approach suggested by an "expert" or a well-intentioned family member. Do what works for your baby and you based on the intimate knowledge you, and only you, have.

Sleep training for your orchid child will be about adjusting environmental conditions and sleep routines and tuning in to your emotional state. Keeping my definition of sleep training in mind, accept that the orchid child will require "just-so" sleep routines. Think about what time of day works best for them and find a way to put some consistent sleep routines in place. Consider also consistency and familiarity when it comes to your child's bathing, changing, and feeding sequences. As part of their "just so" needs, the orchid child will also need you to be particularly attuned to the environmental conditions for sleep. This might include such adjustments as a darkened room, minimal noise, the ideal temperature, the introduction of a soothing noisemaker, and so on. Further, the orchid child is likely to be more reactive to internal upsets such as not feeling well, having a wet or poopy diaper, or gastric reflux, as well as to external upsets such as marital discord or parental anxiety. Think through routine, environmental conditions, and internal and external upsets as you approach the sleep solution for your sensitive, orchid babe.

Your dandelion child may also react to aberrations in the environment, but perhaps to a lesser extent. And the many of you who have children existing at a mid-point somewhere along the orchid-dandelion continuum will need to adjust things according to what works for your child. None of the suggested considerations for an orchid child will negatively affect a dandelion child, or a child who has aspects of both orchid and dandelion. Finding the right routine will take time, patience, and the flexibility to make a change when needed, even if it feels like you've just settled into a routine. As children grow, they change—and so must you.

To Co-Sleep or Not to Co-Sleep?

Alongside the question of whether or not sleep training is safe for babies, the other question I am frequently asked is whether co-sleeping is safe for babies. As with sleep training, my answer is a big old scientifically based "it depends." First, let me clarify some language around co-sleeping. The medical community differentiates between co-sleeping and bedsharing. Co-sleeping is the term used for having your baby in-room with you but not in bed with you. Bedsharing is the term specifically used for having your baby in bed with you.[1]

Since at least 2016, the Canadian Paediatric Society and the American Academy of Pediatrics, along with several other national pediatric organizations around the world, have recommended that infants sleep in the same room as their parents, in a crib or bassinette, for the first six to twelve months of life.[2] The science linked to this recommendation suggests a number of advantages for this arrangement: baby is close by for feeding and settling, and can better sense and be regulated by your presence. Finally, there is the controversial opinion that babies are physically safer when they are in-room *but not in bed* with their parents.

The primary concern over bedsharing is a result of the links between this practice and a coincident rise in baby deaths from sudden infant death syndrome (SIDS) or suffocation.[3] The other concern is the complaint from many parents that having their babies or children in bed or in the room with them is disruptive to their own sleep, leaving them tired and less capable of coping with the demands of parenting and life. And yet, evidence also suggests that the lowest incidence of SIDS occurs in the many cultures and places around the world where co-sleeping and bedsharing is the norm—including southern Europe, Asia, Africa, and Central and South America.[4] Considering these conflicting claims and concerns, you can see where the confusion begins in terms of what parents should and shouldn't do. As it turns out, many parents do bedshare, even in cultures where it is generally deemed unacceptable. But they do so in shame, and they under-report the practice, knowing it is not what they are "supposed" to be doing.[5] This leaning toward bedsharing suggests that parents find it works better, for them and/or for their babies. My advice? Aim for rooming-in as your goal.

With an attachment-focused, developmentally informed approach, the number one concern is always that the baby has the enduring sense that their world is safe, and that the parent can be counted on to meet their needs more often than not. When this is accomplished the baby's regulatory system, and their internal ability to self-soothe back to sleep, will develop exactly as nature intended. So, to bed-share or not? To co-sleep or not? It's a decision you will need to make for yourself, based on the available information. But regardless of the route you take, if you are able to be that available attachment—that ultimate source of safekeeping for your babe—you are on the right path.

Pay Attention to Age and Stage

Most new parents know when they are tired, but it can be harder to recognize the signs of fatigue in babies or young children. Besides parental intuition, age and stage are factors. Newborns are figuring out what it is to simply be in the world, and they have zero capacity for self-soothing. Young children are learning to settle themselves with your help, and will often signal that naptime is needed with their behaviour.

Sleep patterns are highly individual. A young baby will usually settle out at around three naps per day. This may drop down to two naps per day as they approach six months. And roughly around the age of three years, most children will nap only once a day. Variations within these milestones are completely normal. Typically, as a nap falls out of your child's schedule, they may struggle with settling to sleep for a period of time as they transition. Throughout, be sure to watch for your child's sleep cues. Often when a baby or a young child becomes tired, they will turn away from people and their environment to avoid engaging. When that happens, ask yourself if they might be tired and know that an overtired baby will struggle to sleep. Try to hit that sweet spot when your baby is beginning to fatigue and ride the wave into sweet slumber land.

Routines and sleep cues will be an important part of your child's sleep patterns, especially in these early years. Make sure you sculpt those for them with activities leading up to bedtime, such as rocking, singing, and bath time, environmental cues like a darkened room and quiet time, and a full appreciation that it takes the human brain approximately one full hour to go from wide awake to sound asleep.

Non-Attachment-Based Sleep Training

Up to this point, we've talked about how sleep training should be a more adult-focused process. But how did this even become something that parents worry about?

The concept of sleep training emerged in the late twentieth century and was popularized in 1985 with the publication of the well-known and controversial book *Solve Your Child's Sleep Problems* by physician Dr. Richard Ferber. Known as the "Ferber method," and often referred to as "Ferberizing," this approach involved parents leaving their baby to cry for gradually longer periods of time, and not returning to their baby during these periods no matter the amount of crying (the process is also sometimes referred to as controlled crying). The thinking here is that your baby will eventually learn to fall asleep on their own. This is the method my then husband and I attempted to use with our eldest son.

Our son had been sleeping in a bassinette beside our bed, but his dad was becoming more insistent that the baby be moved to his crib in another room. He also was insistent that some version of sleep training should be undertaken because our current arrangement was not "working." You would think, given my background and training, that I would have sorted this out quickly. But the world around me was quite consistent in the message that my chosen path of in-room sleeping and feeding on demand through the night was wrong. Co-sleeping was not a common practice in that day, and one renowned sleep "expert" even told me that by eight weeks, my son needed to be out of our room and in his own crib or I'd risk ruining his sleep habits forever. And so I caved. Off went my baby to his crib in his own room. He didn't sleep well. I didn't sleep well. The discussion between my husband and I took the expected form: Obviously I had made my son too dependent on me. Obviously I had done it wrong. Do you hear the programs at work here? I had an unhappy husband, a baby who wasn't sleeping, and I was exhausted. All around me the chorus was singing that it was time to get on with sleep training.

The dreaded evening arrived when we were to lay my sweet baby's head down to sleep, walk out of the room, close the door, and not return for at least five minutes. Even at the five-minute mark, we were to go in only long enough to settle him and then leave once again. It didn't take long for the crying to start. My gut told me exactly what was needed, which was to go to him, pick him up, and comfort him. But instead, I sat on the floor in the hallway outside the closed door, leaning up against it and willing him to feel my presence through the door. After four minutes of non-stop crying from inside the room, I was sweating profusely and profoundly distressed. And then I found my swagger. The "great mother" rose from somewhere deep inside me. Her presence quieted all the voices—those of the experts and even of my own husband—for nobody messes with the "great mother." She had me on my feet and through that door and scooping up my baby and holding him close. I rocked him and held him and made comforting noises. Soon enough he quieted and drifted off to sleep in my arms, next to my heart, exactly where he needed to be.

Eventually I nestled him into his crib. And, of course, he was awake again a couple hours later. And I was *grateful* to go to him. Grateful for this visit in the quiet of the night. Grateful for the feel of his sweet downy head under my chin. Grateful for the snuggly sensation of his little body cuddled up against mine. I sat in the rocking chair for a long time with him that night. I remember looking out into the star-filled sky and thinking, "There, there, my love. I am here. And all is right in the world again." And that is the story of my sleep-training experience—all four minutes of it.

Besides the Ferber method, there is an even more extreme method of sleep training called "extinction" or "cry it out," made popular by pediatrician Marc Weissbluth in his book *Healthy Sleep Habits, Happy Child.*[6] Often recommended as the quickest way to get your baby sleeping through the night, this method involves you laying your child down in their crib in a separate bedroom, leaving the room, closing the door, and walking away. No intervals. No comforting. Nothing. Sure, your sensitivity to their cries may go extinct, but what is also going extinct here is your child's trust in you, which can impact certain aspects of their ability to grow and develop. This may indeed be the quickest method of sleep training, but is it really what we want for our babies?

Sleep as a Reaction to Stress

Although the sleep-training methods mentioned above appear to work from an outside perspective and in the short term, it is important to understand the impact of such non-attachment-based approaches. For a baby, whose very survival depends on an enduring connection to you, these sleep-training efforts will be experienced as highly stressful. It is worth recalling that stress causes a major dump of cortisol, the stress hormone. As it turns out, cortisol is toxic to the developing brain,[7] and contemporary research has shown that stressing a young child's brain in this way may have a lasting impact on both the physical development of the brain and the emotional development of the child.[8]

So what has enticed parents and experts to use sleep training over the years? It all comes down to appearances. When you sleep train, babies *appear* to sleep better. But it's a misconception. Your baby is not sleeping better. Rather, your baby has become numb to the stress associated with the sleep-training experience. This is a bit like the response of an adult who has experienced a traumatic event. In the midst of the event, the brain goes into alarm mode. If the alarm becomes too intense and/or lasts too long, the human body knows that some level of preservation is required for survival, and shutdown begins. At the extreme end of this numbing, the person will appear spaced out, and then they will go to sleep. This is also why depressed people often experience hypersomnia: sleep is a coping mechanism in the face of high stress.

I once observed a visitation between a mother and her two-year-old girl as part of an ongoing and incredibly acrimonious child-custody dispute. Due to allegations of abuse at the hands of her mother, the child had been raised solely by her father. Unfortunately, forced visitations with the mother had occurred early in the child's life (between the ages of six and twelve months) and without the comforting presence of the known attachment figure—the father. Not surprisingly, these visitations were extremely stressful for this young girl. She often vomited from crying during the weekly two-hour visits. My role was to make a recommendation to the courts regarding the child's well-being and the mother's visitation rights. My first task was to set up a visit between the child and her mother.

The visit began with the child crying as soon as her father walked away. Her crying was intense, and she could not be comforted by her mother, who was essentially unknown to her. The child became increasingly distressed. Her terrified cries soon became whimpers, and her eyes took on a glassy and vacant look. Almost immediately, she fell asleep sitting straight up in her mother's arms, head bobbing off to the side. A few moments later she opened her eyes slightly, cried briefly, and—bam!—off to sleep she went again. When the cycle repeated itself yet again, I swiftly stepped in to end the visit, just twenty minutes after it had begun—and I had the child medically attended to immediately to ensure her well-being in the face of such extraordinary stress.

You see, this child was not sleeping. Her body was shutting down to allow her to survive the extraordinary amount of stress she was experiencing. I offer this example to highlight that the appearance of sleep in the context of traditional sleep training should not be thought of as success. Since babies have not yet developed the neurological wiring necessary for self-regulation, they will be forced into a "sleep" state when their underdeveloped brains are toxically stressed by disruptions in the parent-child bond. And that is essentially the definition of non-attachment-based sleep-training approaches, particularly cry-it-out methods.

"Self-Soothing" is a Myth

Another long-held belief in the sleep-training camp is that babies must "learn" how to self-soothe. The benchmark is that by around six weeks of age your baby should be sleeping through the night. If she isn't, then it's time to sleep train so that you can teach her how. The problem with this, neurologically speaking, is that self-regulation—or the capacity to self-soothe back to sleep—is non-existent in the infant brain. It is akin to asking a three-year-old to print their name neatly or expecting a five-year-old to easily break down the task of "clean your room" into steps. The neural infrastructure needed to support self-soothing is simply unavailable to an infant.

Some observers may point out that lots of babies do sleep through the night, and from an early age. That may be true, but those babies are not sleeping through the night because they're rock-star self-regulators. They are sleeping because the conditions within and/or around them are highly conducive to them sleeping. They might be more settled and sorted in terms of their natural temperament. They might be easygoing dandelion babes, for example. Or perhaps their parents are settled, and there is very little stress or marital strife present in the home. Or perhaps there are no other siblings making noise and demanding attention.

The non-sleeping babies are not sleeping because the conditions within and/or around them are not conducive. Maybe they aren't feeling well. Maybe they have gastroesophageal reflux disease, as so many babies do. Maybe they are orchid babies, which means they are hyper-alert to all that is going on around them. Maybe there are other things happening in their little world that have heightened the stress in the air of their home. Some of these conditions will be changeable; many of them won't. Sleep "training" should focus only on what is changeable. The rest will develop in good time and as nature intended.

The Sleep Survival Guide for Exhausted Parents

You cannot spoil your baby or young child with love and presence and safe-care. If you feel as if sleep has become an area of challenge for you in growing your little babe, here is a sleep survival guide that will have both of you thriving. Sweet dreams!

- Sleep training is for adults. Adults—not children—must adjust the things within their control that may be affecting their child's sleep. This includes environmental conditions, your child's temperament and internal states, routines around sleep, and your emotional state.
- For babies younger than six months, think of every cry as an emergency. Go to them every time. No forced separations. No imposed intervals of crying.

- If you are depleted, make sure your baby is physically safe and walk away to settle yourself. Get help from another caregiver if one is available.
- Co-sleeping, also known as rooming-in—having your baby sleeping in a bassinette or crib beside you—is the recommended approach for babies aged up to six to twelve months.
- Bedsharing with your baby is not recommended by experts due to the higher incidence of SIDS correlated with this practice.
- Figure out what time of day works best for your child to sleep and cater to that, especially if you have an orchid-type baby or young child.
- Honour routine, especially sequences that precede sleep—such as bathing, changing, and feeding—that will help your baby's internal monitoring systems sense that sleep is on the horizon.
- Tinker with routine to find what works for your child. This will take time, patience, and the ability to make a change when needed. Step into all of this with swagger.
- Dissect your internal stories and programs and redirect your energy to your child's needs while affirming your own needs.
- Remember always that "normal" sleep patterns are unique to the individual child and are affected by your child's age, temperament, and environment.
- Infants sleep more than toddlers. Toddlers sleep more than preschoolers. But preschoolers are better than toddlers at amalgamating their sleep into long stretches.
- With every change in sleep routine, anticipate some upset in the sleep habits of your child. With consistent care this upset should eventually settle out.

7

FEEDING AND EATING

FOR MANY PARENTS, feeding can be an all-consuming child-hood issue. This is especially true in the first precious years of life, when you want to make sure your child gets the nutrition they need in order to grow healthily. But all of this intense focus on and worry about food can create a hotbed of challenges, as eating is intimate stuff. Remember how important it is that you are full of swagger for your little one (see chapter 4)? When swagger is surrendered to worry, things are bound to go sideways. In this chapter I will talk about how feeding contributes to the relationship dance that supports your child's development. Place your trust in this process and you can step confidently into your provider role as you nourish your baby's body and sense of self.

Babies and Breastfeeding

Connection around feeding is vitally important for infant development. Whether you are breast- or bottle-feeding, when you feed your baby in your arms they are located at the perfect distance to see your face clearly. Babies don't see well, but the human baby has evolved to see a parent's face and eyes when held at arm's length. So, when your baby looks to you while being fed, make sure they are seeing your eyes. If you are looking at your phone (something researchers and child development specialists now refer to as "brexting"), or are busy chatting, or otherwise distracted, your baby will be gazing at your chin or your earlobe—that isn't even in the same universe as the power of connection through eye-to-eye contact.

Not only does your baby benefit from the feeding time as an opportunity for connection over and over again, but you benefit too. As you breastfeed you baby, your body secretes a wash of hormones designed specifically to support your parent-baby bond.[1] If you are bottle-feeding, this time of togetherness and connection will similarly be incredibly powerful and will release you to a space of emotional rest where you are able to feel deeply connected to your little one. So be sure to honour feeding time with your baby as an opportunity for contact and closeness. You can do so knowing that the connection you foster will be soaked up through his senses and consolidated in his brain as a deep experience of regulation, and in his developing sense of self as a little person who is worthy of love and affection. What power!

Introducing Solids

Contemporary approaches to the introduction of solid foods espouse baby-led weaning and feeding.[2] The thinking is that your baby will know how much is enough, what works for them, and what they are ready for. Outdated approaches often advise weaning baby according to a schedule or to suit an adult.

In the world of attachment-focused parenting, there are no goalposts where cessation of breastfeeding is concerned—that idea is an entirely culturally derived phenomenon. There are some parts of the world where breastfeeding is an absolute must well into early childhood or the child may die from starvation or malnutrition. In

North America, social policies around lengths of maternity and parental leaves play a huge role. And stigma drives most parents to end breastfeeding long before either they or the child is ready. I believe wholeheartedly that the parent is the guide, and by being intuitively attuned to the cues of the child, will capably find their way through this transition.

From an attachment perspective, the problem with these outdated approaches around when to stop breastfeeding is that they aren't about truly seeing and hearing your baby. If your baby still wants to nurse, and you are wondering if they're getting too old for this, check in with the See It, Feel It, Be It process outlined in chapter 4:

- **See It:** My baby is still nursing and I am not sure if this is okay.

- **Feel It Me:** What is happening? Am I worried about the judgments of others? Am I anxious for my own time and for my body to be restored to me? What stories might be lurking behind this anxiety? (For example, did you ever feel invaded as a child or as though your needs were not honoured or met?)

- **Feel It Child:** What is happening for my baby? Do they need this connected time because they miss me while I am at work? Have there been changes in my child's world that they might have difficulty coping with? Is nursing providing a good dose of regulation for them?

- **Be It:** Step in and do what is right for your child. Keep on nursing if that is what you are pulled toward. Stop if it is not. Above all, inform your decision from unimpeded instinct rather than story.

Once you begin the exciting period of introducing solids to your baby, your core job is to provide a wide variety of healthy foods prepared in a manner that is safe, and then guide them as they sort through what to do with that food. Jennifer House writes extensively about this in her *Parents' Guide to Baby-Led Weaning,* as do Dr. Gill Rapley and Tracey Murkett in *Baby-led Weaning: Helping Your Baby to Love Good Food.* Among others, these are the experts on this process, and they have lots of ideas for how to begin the transition to solid food.

When you are full of swagger, your energy will suggest to your baby that this change in their life is all well and good. Follow these simple directives to deliver the experienced message that your baby is seen and heard throughout. No forcing or cajoling or demanding.

- Let your baby play with and explore their food.
- Let them watch you around food as you sit and eat a family meal together.
- Make the act of preparing food and feeding your baby one that is full of ritual and love—this simple approach absolutely places you in the lead position.
- If baby indicates they are finished with their food, be the kind of big person that sees that, gets it, and puts it away for now.
- If baby indicates an intense dislike of a specific food, accept that they don't need to eat it right now. Present that food at other sittings as necessary. Your child will gradually increase their food repertoire with the safety of knowing none of this is a power play.

As your baby progresses from eating offered foods in the high chair to sitting at the table, consider how you can make this a smooth transition so your baby knows you are in the lead.

- Have your baby sit in your lap or close to you at the table so that all-important physical proximity is part of the feeding experience.
- Provide your baby with options so they can explore a range of foods and be sure to include one or two foods you know she

enjoys—this will give your little foodie the message that you support her in her adventures.

- As your child gets older and sits more independently at the family table, consider serving your meals family style, where food is placed in the middle of the table and everybody either serves themselves or indicates to an adult what they would like to be served.
- Always include one thing on the table that you know your child will enjoy—and trust their gut!

Feeding Challenges in Babies

With babies, there are two areas where parents might confront challenges. One is with breastfeeding and the other is with the introduction of solids.

Breastfeeding Struggles

Breastfeeding comes more easily to some than others, but it's a learned experience for all new mothers and there are bound to be initial challenges. Give yourself the time to settle into a rhythm. Lisa Carleton, an International Board Certified Lactation Consultant, has worked with hundreds of parents around challenges with breastfeeding, and her advice is that it can take four to six weeks (and sometimes longer) to feel recovered and settled about breastfeeding. Lactation consultants like Carleton understand that issues with the shape and size of an individual woman's breast may make it more challenging for a mother to get that perfect latch. Some babies have small mouths or tongue ties—when their tongues are attached too firmly to the bottom of their mouths—that can prevent the movement needed for easy breastfeeding. The "hamburger" nipples that result from improper latching can make breastfeeding painful and make the process of feeding your baby one full of anguish. Carleton very strongly suggests seeking qualified help if you are struggling with breastfeeding issues in the first few weeks or even beyond. The sooner you get support, the sooner those challenges will be resolved, and the sooner you will be affirmed in your confident swagger as you move forward.

If you have struggled with breastfeeding, be aware that an uneasy emotional loop can often be created as a result. When a mother feels as if she is failing at something that is supposed to be so natural, unease can settle in and create huge waves of upset. This upset will almost certainly leave your child feeling more agitated, adding additional challenge to the feeding connection. Breastfeeding doesn't always work the way moms and babies want it to, and that's perfectly okay. There are other options—such as pumping and bottle-feeding or formula bottle-feeding—that do work. You may find the support of a lactation consultant or other professional helpful in determining what is going to work for you. If that means moving on from breastfeeding to bottle-feeding, know that your child will be fine. And so will you.

Typically, the emotional complexities of nursing may follow from and complicate a situation that began with physical issues. When you are trying to give your baby life-sustaining milk and it hurts or doesn't seem to be working, it's no surprise that anxiety can result. As challenges surface with breastfeeding, so too can challenges emerge in the mother-baby bond. These are usually born of the mother's concern that she hasn't done a good enough job or that the baby isn't taking to feeding and therefore may not be taking to her. These stories can feel devastating, and they set up a challenging cycle of mom being upset, baby being upset, and feeding getting hijacked. There is enormous power in knowing that these are just stories, the result of your programming and attempts to rush forward during this time of feeling triggered and stressed.

Throughout this journey take note of your internal programs as they surface: Not good enough. Doing it wrong. Not worthy. Programs, each and every one. Be gracious with yourself and empathetic with your baby as you sort through the struggle. And know you are not alone. A lot of moms and babies have a hard go with this, and there is help available.

Refusing Solids

The transition from nursing to solids also takes patience and attention to your internal stories and programs, especially if your child wants to continue breastfeeding (see page 143). If you're concerned that your baby isn't getting enough food because he is refusing solids, know that a bottle and breastfeeding will get them through on a day when the food show simply isn't happening. Play around with different flavours and textures to see what your baby prefers.

If you are concerned that the avoidance of solids is a bigger issue, consult with appropriate professionals who can guide you to make sure your baby gets what she needs. Food avoidance issues in young babies may involve sensory challenges (the texture or flavour of food is experienced as exceedingly offensive to the child), a swallowing issue, or some other physical roadblock that is in the way of a smooth transition to solids.

Your emotional state has a significant impact on your baby, and especially so around feeding time. Maybe even more so than adults, babies and small children are instinctually wired to be keenly attuned to the minutiae of your cues. They are not actually thinking, "Uh-oh, Mom/Dad is having a bad day; I'd better get ready for the storm," but their neurons will be quivering in anticipation.

If you are overwhelmed, anxious, or depressed, your baby is going to feel it. Maybe you are predisposed to feeling anxious, or perhaps there are heightened financial pressures or work challenges on your shoulders. Regardless of the reason for your uncomfortable feelings, babies are super-sensors, and orchid babies are super-sensors to the power of infinity, which means your baby's system will always be on high alert, ready for possible disconnection. Sort out what programs have been triggered within you as a result of re-entering the intimate space of the parent-child dynamic, and specifically with respect to feeding.

Are your feelings of anxiety, depression, or being overwhelmed directly related to feeding? Maybe your emotional and/or physical needs around feeding were not met when you were a child. Or are these feelings arising from a more general level of worry, such as panic around knowing that another human is entirely dependent on you? Are you concerned that you might mess your child up? That they might hate you for doing a terrible job? Do you feel that you are not a good parent?

Check in with and walk through these feelings. Focus on how you can reassure your inner child that all is well so you can help your baby know that all is well too. Feeding yourself a new narrative that has a more positive storyline can relieve the pressure and make feeding your child an easier, more fulfilling experience for both of you.

Feeding Toddlers and Young Children

As your baby grows into a toddler and gets the hang of eating solids, it is important that you read your child's cues and provide accordingly. Your little one wants to know that you get them, that you are a safe, kind big person who can be counted on. You want your child to lean into your safe embrace when it comes to food. Making a young child sit at the table for endless amounts of time, demanding they follow "adult" rules or feed themselves, does not place you in the lead. Instead, you are defecting from any kind of safe leadership role. Dependence is the true path to independence.

Stepping in confidently for your growing little human is the ticket. Feeding your child can deepen the foundational relationship you have with them. Here is some practical information and a few ideas to guide you in making this a positive experience.

Encourage, Explore, Embrace

- Encourage the exploring of food and offer many opportunities to taste-test new foods. Children often need multiple exposures to unfamiliar foods before feeling comfortable enough to try them.
- Cook for your children, allow them to help you when they can, and cater to their likes.
- Share appropriate guidelines for dinner table expectations, but don't enforce them with military precision.
- Feed children when they need it. Let them feed themselves when they want to. Let them explore and practise with utensils as their fine motor skills develop.
- Embrace the big, beautiful mess!

Adjust the Environment

- Create routines full of connection and incorporate cues for young children so that they know when and how meals are about to take place—adjust as needed as they grow and change. Your child will enjoy the emotional rest when they know when meals are arriving and what they will be eating. An orchid child will be far more amenable when you take this approach.
- Think about your at-home routines and on-the-road routines. There will be occasions when you need to feed your child on the run. You can still build in routine to that on-the-fly meal with the

rollout of a favourite picnic blanket, a favourite placemat, or a mealtime song. When setting your routines for feeding consider what part of that routine is transportable to help your child settle while eating on the go.

Connect in Calm

- Reserve mealtime as sacred for connection to your child and family. Put away phones and turn off other devices. We are meant to break bread as families and enjoy the communality of the meal. And children are meant to be nurtured by their parents in the act of food preparation and provision. Research shows that families who eat dinner together most of the time have children who have lower challenges with mental health issues.[3]
- Make the meal table a calm, peaceful one so that children can settle into the act of eating. Engage in some mindfulness practices to quiet your own emotional charge. Create some rituals around how you gather, how you give thanks, and how you connect as a family over a meal.

Feeding Challenges in Toddlers and Young Children

Whenever there is a persistent feeding issue with your child that has you concerned, a professional assessment can determine if there is some other difficulty at play. Children need to be properly assessed and diagnosed by the appropriate professional in case they have swallowing challenges or difficulties with processing sensory information related to food.

Physical Challenges

Physical difficulties can make it hard for young children to figure out how to swallow food. In some children, the muscles in the mouth and throat may not be working properly, and support may be required to get things moving. This support could take the form of physical or occupational therapy, or even surgery. Other physical issues, such as scarring from serious reflux disorders, may restrict how much food a child can swallow, or result in food being vomited back up. Extreme sensory issues, including sensory processing disorder involving taste, texture, and/or smell, can readily stimulate the gag reflex for a child, making eating an unpleasant experience that they desperately—and determinedly!—want to avoid. Pediatric occupational therapists are often well versed in feeding challenges that stem from sensory issues. If you end up needing the support of outside professionals, know that it is essential that you are in the lead of these supports and that your child never experiences consequences connected to how they eat.

Psychological and Emotional Challenges

Though there are medical or physical issues that can interrupt feeding, emotional and psychological issues may also be at play. Struggles with eating in young children can be born out of a power dynamic. Your child knows how important eating well is for you and may decide that this is where he is going to take a stand. Every parent out there knows that even if you succeed in getting food into a child's mouth, you cannot make them swallow it. And if it does go down, it can always come back up.

If your child has become picky about eating or is having trouble eating, and you've determined that it is not a physical issue, consider the following possibilities:

- Your child simply doesn't like specific flavours or textures.
- Your child is sensitive, and a disruption to their routine is setting them off.
- Your child finds the environment too busy, and it is distracting them from eating.
- Your child is sensing an emotionally charged atmosphere, and it is winding them up.

Determine carefully which of these issues you control and use your expert knowledge of your child to confidently adjust the environment around them.

Since the act of eating is deeply intimate and involves significant vulnerability, it is not uncommon to see power struggles play out between child and parent and/or caregiver. Forcing food on a child should be avoided. You can put food in a child's mouth, but you cannot make them swallow it without a horrid and emotionally damaging power struggle. When you force your children to eat food they hate, you are not in the lead. You are childishly far behind. This type of situation shines light on your ineptitude in choosing a battle you cannot possibly win and will only escalate into additional battles, which may spill over from the dinner table into the rest of life.

Children may turn to food as an easy source of control should they sense it lapsing in other places. Some children will restrict food intake in an effort to feel in control of their lives. Ask yourself: What are the conditions in your child's life that might be leading them to feel that they lack control? What can you do to calm your child's storm and bring order and peace back into the picture as their more enduring experience? Instead of battling symptoms, find the root source. Think of the contributing picture, work swiftly and confidently to adjust, and watch the food challenges lessen.

One way that a child might enact control through food is when they connect being fed to being calmed. Sometimes this connection may become the go-to for addressing feelings of anxiety and upset—that is, food becomes the substitute for attachment with a capable caregiver or parent. When the child eats, they get an initial rush of feeling better emotionally. Problematically, however, the child is using food to fill their tummies when what needs filling is their heart. Rather than more food, the child needs more connection and more access to experiences of being calmed by their big person.

I worked with a three-year-old boy who refused food unless his mother placed it directly into his mouth. His family had recently gone through a huge ordeal, emigrating from a war-torn homeland. The little boy was overwhelmed, anxious, and had many challenging experiences to process. He figured out a way to build a resolute brain bridge (see page 64) to his mother by getting her to feed him by hand, which allowed him to stay close to her. This family needed some time to feel safe in their new home and country. The mother needed to get her bearings and feel her natural swagger return. And this little boy needed to be able to lean in, deeply dependent, for a good long while on the certain safety and care of his parents. The solution was not to stop the mother from feeding her son, but to encourage her to do this before he asked for it and to simultaneously build in other sources of connectivity between them through caregiving routines, play, and in everyday life.

Most power struggles are the result of a child attempting to take the lead from an adult who the child perceives is not fully in control of the child's world. This perception, whether accurate or not, alarms the child, and food may become involved as a source of control and even substitute connection. The root cause of this power struggle may or may not have anything to do with food. Keep in mind that you can be the best parent ever, but if control of a situation (a painful medical procedure endured by the child, for example, or an unavoidable separation that was too long and intense) is what has caused your child to waver in their personal belief of safety, you are the one your child knows to turn to. That is the way nature set it up. You are the big person and are perfectly positioned to answer this call.

EATING SHOULD BE a joyful and connected affair full of ease for both you and your child. It does not need to be a battleground. It does not need to be full of worry and angst. Yes, there can be challenges. But as soon as those pop up, know that you have the ready script of See It, Feel It, Be It to help you work through them. With a solid sense of confidence and know-how, get to work. Seek support as you need it, see and hear your child always, cherish feeding for the opportunity it presents to connect with your growing child, and watch their body be nourished along with their heart.

8

TOILET TRAINING

ONE OF THE big moments of your little's life will be the day she learns to use the toilet. It will be a big thing for both of you. I remember clearly the day this happened for my first-born. We were buying furniture at an enormous big-box store. I would have preferred that he pee in his diaper or out in the car, where I had a portable potty stowed in case this moment arose. But it happened in a public washroom that I imagined was covered in germs and filth! And, of course, he wanted to sit down to make it all happen, "just like Mommy." As my son gripped the toilet bowl he proudly and loudly exclaimed over his feat so everyone in that washroom also got to experience his first big pee in the potty. You could hear the soft giggles and exclamations from the other moms. My boy then hopped down and wanted to high-five me multiple times with, yes, his germy, filthy, toilet-bowl hands. Perfect! I got to work on my programming about that, we both went in for the celebration, and then promptly did some serious hand washing.

The path to toilet training is unique to each child. Although there is not much you can or should do to hurry up nature, here are some general guidelines to help your growing little navigate the wonderful world of pee and poo in the toilet bowl.

When to start toilet training: Toilet training begins when the child shows an interest in related behaviours and when their diapers seem to stay dry for about two hours at a time. Daytime toilet training usually happens before nighttime toilet training, which means that even if your child is managing during the day, they may still use diapers at night. Given that their interest is key to the toileting process, don't be shy about your little one hanging around the bathroom while you take care of your own business. This curiosity is a good clue that your child is ready to emulate that behaviour and figure out the control of their bowels and bladder. Sometimes parents worry that being naked or partially undressed around a young child is a bad thing. That is a story coming from your own programming. Your young child doesn't care what you are wearing or not. The time to be sensitive is when your child does not want to be naked in front of you. Stories about sexualized nakedness aside, if you are concerned that your child is not displaying any curiosity about toileting, be diligent about reading children's storybooks on the topic, talk openly about toileting for yourself and for them, and start to encourage peeing and pooping on the potty as an idea for them to mull over.

Helpful ways to begin: Begin by sitting your child on the toilet at regular intervals to see if you catch them voiding in the toilet. Try at least once an hour and as frequently as once every twenty minutes if that doesn't work. You might use a child-sized potty or consider a step stool and insert for your toilet, as many children feel unstable when sitting atop the opening built for adult-sized bottoms. You can choose to let your child go without diapers on days when you are home. If you do, expect spillage and overflow as a normal part of that process and be ready to manage cleanup without worry and hurry. Or you might decide to go a less intense route and keep a diaper on your child and be diligent with regular sittings on the potty.

How long should it take? This will be different for each child depending on their age level, gender, level of sensitivity, how divided their attention is, and what is happening around the home. Most children get interested in toileting around two years of age, but some children, my own included, don't give it a second thought until three years. Some research suggests that boys take up the toilet-training torch later than girls.[1] If you have a little boy, it is possible that your son's start time may be later than your own girls or your friends' daughters.

If you have a highly sensitive orchid child, the toilet training may happen quickly because the child's sensitivity to wet diapers or wet clothing is high and they are motivated to avoid this yucky feeling. Alternatively, toilet training can be delayed because the orchid child's mind is distracted by external stimuli (noise, light, heat, energy), leaving little room to recognize when they feel the need to use the potty. Finally, if there are big changes happening in your child's life—such as the birth of a sibling, the start of preschool, a divorce or the introduction of a new partner, the death of a pet, or a move—understand that these changes may either delay the start of successful toilet training or lead to a bit of a setback; for example, your child may have more accidents until things settle. This happens because children experience and express dysregulation through their bodies. The sensations of having to urinate or defecate might not be as prevalent in a storm of dysregulation brought about by changes or emotional upset. During these times, children may express more infantile behaviour so they will be cared for and thus regulated.

Normalizing Accidents

Regardless of the circumstances around your child's potty accident, there is absolutely no place for shame or blame in the raising of a child at any time. If pee or poo hit the floor or your couch instead of the toilet, seek to normalize the experience for your child. "It is so hard to hold onto your pee sometimes, isn't it, love?" or "Sometimes your poo just sneaks out, doesn't it?" Carry on with the reassuring message that you know exactly what to do and finish by planting a seed of ability for the next time. "Next time you can try again to poo in the toilet. You will get it one day. I know you will!"

If you go the route of blame and shame, you may successfully frighten or bully your child into making sure their business has landed in the toilet more quickly, but there is a price to pay. Best not to deny your little one access to an essential need—connection—to secure performance or a preferred behaviour of any kind. Preserve your child's dignity and make sure they are comfortable. No need to draw big attention to any accidents. Instead, quietly lead your child through it so they can rest in your care. Help your child with simple, thoughtful gestures such as packing clean bottoms and underwear in their school backpack, or keeping a spare set in the car.

There is something wonderfully settling for kids when they see their own story on the pages of a book. During the early days of toilet training look for books or stories that talk about accidents happening, that explain that these are part of learning, and that also carry the message of connection as a core theme. But I caution you here to steer clear of books or other messages that are full of reward systems or that use "big girl" or "big boy" kind of language. The underlying message here is that the child who has an accident is not deserving of the reward or is not big enough. For some reason, the toilet-training world is full of this blame and shame rhetoric. Vet these messages and weed out the negative talk before it is absorbed by your child. Also available are some lovely online videos that you can show a child who is three years of age or older. Ask your health care practitioner for up-to-date recommendations, or do some research yourself to find sources that resonate with you.

Routine and Consistency

If your child knows what is going to happen around toileting, then the likelihood that they will come along for the ride is much higher. I strongly recommend having some routines around how you handle toileting. Timing is especially important. Does your child sit on the potty when they wake up, before they go to bed, and right before or after each meal? Do you have a timer set for sitting your child down on that potty at least every hour, or as often as recommended by your health care provider? Your child isn't going to track this timing, so you will need to lead this. As you do, understand that it is hard for your child to pause doing the things they love to go to the bathroom. Use heart and empathy around their upset, but hold the line. Even though they might resist, there will be rest for them in knowing that all they need do is lean into your capable care.

Another part of routine and consistency is being ready for toileting when you are away from home. Here are some suggestions to make that happen smoothly:

- Get a mobile potty that you can pop in the back of the car for use when the timer goes off and you are on the road, or when your child indicates they need to go.

- Pack what you need for your child to comfortably use public toilets, such as a child-sized toilet seat that fits over the bowl. Toilet bowl openings are big for little bums; your child's little hands will be gripping that toilet seat, so plan how you will manage that.

- Plan for the dreaded automatic toilet flush that can sound like a jet plane taking off. This can be intensely frightening, especially for a sensitive orchid child. Consider that toileting is vulnerable stuff for a little one. You don't want them to be terrified when they need to be as settled as possible. To avoid that automatic-flush *whoosh*, carry around a pad of sticky notes or something else opaque and sticky that you can place overtop of the sensor behind the auto-flush toilet.

"Samesies"

One of the ways little kids feel connected to their big people is by finding the "samesies" they share. A basic premise of social psychology is that we tend to like people with whom we share common ground. By the second year of their life, your little one will become deeply invested in being the same as you. As a parent, you can make this desire work in the toileting process—they can pee or poo in the toilet, "just like Mommy/Daddy." You can model for them. If you are a single mom with a little boy, you might find a trusted male role model to act as a substitute in showing your kiddo how it all works. And if you are a single dad with a little girl, you might find a trusted female role model to do the same.

Make It Fun!

The more you can inject joy and playfulness into learning things that are or have become tricky, the better it will be emotionally for your child. This approach will also likely quicken the conquering of the difficulty. There is an old Finnish saying that, roughly translated, means "what is learned without joy is soon forgotten." So, amplify and accelerate learning by having your child land on joy while learning how to use the toilet. Maybe you have funny songs you sing together while sitting on the toilet. Maybe your little boy gets to aim at cereal O's in the bowl. Use fun to create connection and emotional rest so your child can *release*, literally and figuratively. As they do, they will figure out how their elimination systems work for them, and in the process, they will be able to lean into you, allowing you to take charge so they don't have to.

Avoid Reward Systems

I talk to parents a lot about the downside of using rewards when trying to encourage children to fall into line. I'm talking about handing out stickers and candies and the promise of a toy after five stars earned on the reward chart for successful toileting. I call the downside to a reward system the "no-reward system." Though a reward system might be fun when your child gets a reward, when they fall short and do not get that reward, they experience frustration and even emotional disconnect from you. Furthermore, a reward system keeps the focus on external motivation rather than allowing the child to connect with their internal needs. How can children come to know their bodies, their urges, and themselves over time if we surround them with approaches that involve listening to the outside and performing for rewards? Not taking the rewards approach means that development may take a little longer, but children should not be rushed. Allow them to take their time while learning how to manage toileting themselves.

Change Your Story

Your child peed all over the couch. Your child pooped in their clothes. Again. How much longer will you have to tolerate this? It is so much work! Sound familiar? When your child is working to figure out toilet training and has some accidents along the way, and you lament that it is happening with a big wish to have it be done already, you are arguing with reality. Keep on with this approach and, as Byron Katie says, "You will be wrong, but only 100% of the time."[2]

Our lives would change if we truly accepted what is, rather than arguing with reality. When you create an alternate reality that you think *should* be your reality—such as "My child should NOT be peeing all over the couch!" or "My child should NOT be pooping in their pants still"—and thinking about it causes you to become upset, you create stress. If you accept your reality, you resolve that stress. How does this approach work when you are helping your child with toileting? As you support your child along the path of development, come alongside them from a place of neutrality at the least, and maybe even from a place of full acceptance, so as to not inject stress into the environment. When you accept reality you get to be at peace, and your child rests in this calm energy and is released to the task of figuring out toileting rather than being muddled by your upset.

When Toilet Training is a Challenge

Challenges with toileting can be multi-faceted, and that often puzzles parents. Knowing how to best support your child with toileting issues is first about making a distinction: What is developmental, and will therefore resolve naturally as maturation proceeds and with some caring support, and what is potentially the result of physical and/or emotional causes?

But how does one even begin navigating this? You begin as you do in all things with parenting—by sitting in a calm place of confident swagger knowing that you've got this, even when you are still sorting it out. Believe that everything experienced by you and your child along the way is perfect. Consider other possible contributors to the situation (changes in your child's environment, for example), and go through the appropriate steps of checking in on things medically.

Too Busy to Go

Sometimes a child's mind is too busy to deal with the focus required to manage peeing and pooing. This means that overflow is not a control issue as much as it is an issue of brain maturation. The brain will mature; in the meantime, you can offer your child some support around routines with reminders. Children who are bright often fall into the "too busy to go" category because their intelligent minds do not pay attention to what is happening in their body when they are busy attending to many other things. One of the downsides of being bright is that the brain is constantly absorbing extraneous information. This makes a kid smart but ultimately more distractible.

Compared to their same-aged peers, children who are struggling with attention issues, or attentional control, can also have difficulties with bowel and bladder overflow. Poo or pee can slip out, usually unnoticed, and they carry on playing with whatever engrossed them in the first place. Attentional control can be a challenge for young children for two reasons—one developmental and the other emotional. It is important to understand that children under the age of six are designed to be inattentive. The frontal and prefrontal cortical regions of the brain that regulate attentional systems do not come online until a child is six or seven years of age. Brain development, however, is unique from one child to the next, so it is not uncommon to see differences in development. These differences should not raise red flags immediately, but it's worth noting that when a child appears to be behind compared to other children in terms of attention, this lag may interfere with toilet training. The developmental reason for the lag might simply be that this child's brain is taking longer to develop in the attentional areas.

Another reason for attentional challenges is that the child has experienced some upsetting events, past or present, and this has caused their brain to be in scan-and-search mode rather than in focused-and-targeted mode. Instead of zeroing in on specific tasks, the brain is on the lookout for danger. Scan-and-search mode is instinctively activated in a child in an act of self-preservation when something upsetting has settled into their psyche. Upset launches them into a period of stress, hypervigilance, and fight-or-flight responding. If the child has experienced something traumatic or is living through upsetting events—such as loss (death, separation/ divorce, adoption, foster care), relationship disruption, discord in the home, and life changes like new siblings, a new partner for Mom or Dad, or a move to a new home and/or daycare—their brains might be otherwise focused. Paying attention to body cues in the middle of these changes can be more fleeting. As the child's emotional distress is processed and lessens, the attentional networks can once again become more focused, allowing for the toilet training to settle down.

Do You Feel You Need to Go?

Another developmental contributor to toilet training is the individual child's internal abilities regarding sensory processing. When we think of the senses, sight, hearing, smell, taste, and touch are the ones that automatically come to mind. But humans also have internal sensation systems that often don't get talked about, and one of these is called our interoceptive system. Interoception is the sense we have about what is going on inside our body. Are we thirsty? Or hot? Or hungry? Interoception also includes the ability to sense and attend to the body's urge for elimination. Since this is a brain-based activity, when there is an issue with interoception, it usually involves how different parts of the brain are communicating with each other rather than a "problem" with any one specific part of the brain. Pediatric occupational therapists can be incredibly helpful in sorting through this with parents and providing strategies for stimulating brain growth and positive development.

In this case, what's important to understand is that the inability to sense the urge to eliminate is not wilful on the part of your child. This is a "can't do" rather than a "won't do." She literally does not sense the urge. Like all children with either developmental or emotionally based toilet-training struggles, this child will need support and encouragement to understand their body and their cues. Having a parent who is lovingly in charge and leading the way will be key.

Emotional Trauma

I once worked with a family who came in to see me because their five-year-old boy was unable to poo in the toilet. He had pee down just fine, but pooing was a battle. He would sneak off to corners of the house and secretly defecate. Or sneak a diaper out of the cupboard, pull down his underpants, put on the diaper, and poo into it. If he was made to sit down on the potty to poo he would cry and most times would become angry.

As it turned out, this period in his life was not the only distressing one. His developmental history revealed that he had been ill at twelve months of age. Initially his illness was diagnosed as a flu bug, but after several days of vomiting and lethargy, he collapsed in his mother's arms. They raced off to emergency at a local hospital only to be airlifted to the nearest children's hospital. Within hours this little boy was having brain surgery to remove a substantial tumour that reportedly had been growing since he was in utero. The parents were told his chances of surviving the surgery were 50 percent, and so they said their goodbyes in case he didn't make it. But he did survive, and he is now a happy, healthy, thriving kid. However, this entire experience was terribly traumatic for him and his parents.

Thankfully, this little boy's recovery went relatively smoothly. Although he has some lasting learning differences, there was no major brain damage that would have had a direct impact on toileting. However, in my experience with families who have lived through similar types of situations, the emotional challenge can make it difficult to carry on as before. In the soup of all that trauma, relationships can take a hit. This boy's family was no different. When I met this child at the age of five, his parents' relationship was on the rocks, and they divorced within the year.

Along the way, the boy needed some way to feel in control of a life that must have felt beyond his control at times. His body was out of sorts. His emotions were running on high, causing him to be vigilant and sensitive to everything. And his parents were struggling. They had been ever since his surgery at the age of twelve months. What is a little boy to do? Simple. Manifest some version of control by holding on to his poo. Letting his poo fall out of his body down into a toilet was like letting go of himself, and that was a terrifying prospect.

Anxiety

Sometimes young children express heightened levels of anxiety even without causal trauma. This might be because they are highly sensitive orchid children. Or maybe their anxiety is an acute response to a life event or change that might not be traumatic but is still unsettling. And when life feels out of control, a child cannot rest easy in that directionless wasteland. Unfortunately, if a child looks around and senses that life isn't safe and manageable and controllable, they will move themselves into the control position. Holding onto pee and poo is a natural way to be in control.

One four-year-old girl I worked with fit exactly into this category. Her parents were both professionals who worked long hours, and she struggled being away from them in daycare. She was bright and sensitive, and had to deal with a bunch of noisy kids all day away from the comforts of home and her parents—she was overwhelmed.

She was struggling with going to sleep, had lots of meltdowns before and after daycare, and had smears and bits of poo in her underwear constantly. The intervention used in her case had little to do with finding a physical reason for her bowel overflow and more to do with settling her anxiety.

Regardless of how a child's overflow issues begin, sustained bowel overflow has some longer-term complications. The bowels can become distended, and the sensors in the bowels that would normally signal to a child's brain that it is time to poop can go numb. Altogether this results in difficulties in the mechanics of pushing out their poo and the capacity to know when it is time to poo. Instead, it just slips out in little smears and nuggets that you will be cleaning up endlessly, rather than one neat, tidy bowel movement. Your health care practitioner can talk you through options for allowing the bowel to return to its normal shape and function.

Unprocessed trauma or emotional upset can be a significant contributor to overflow, especially bowel overflow. Control is at the heart of it all, and understanding this can make the situation more approachable when it comes to finding solutions. It can be complex, however, and often requires time, patience, and a whole lot of love to get it turned around.

Finding a Solution

Most children will progress through toilet training with parents using typical approaches and without a whiff of unusual challenge. But when things go sideways and your child struggles with ongoing bowel or bladder overflow, that's when you need to support your child in a different way. I have supported many families through this kind of a challenge. I purchased furniture for my clinic space that is meant to appear cozy and inviting and is easily cleaned. Usually the overflow is stuff that trickles out, that rolls down pant legs, or that smears out from under dresses, rather than a big puddle of pee or a pile of poop. In the world of child psychology, this is standard fare, so if your child has a challenge in this area, rest assured that you are in good company and this is conquerable.

As there are various anatomical and medical explanations for overflow challenges, you should first explore those contributors with your medical practitioner. You will want to rule out anatomical aberrations and other things that can get in the way of having toileting go smoothly for your little one. From there, the problem must be viewed through one of two lenses. The first lens is differences in development that might make toilet training difficult for your child. The second lens circles around emotional upset. It's also possible to have toileting challenges that result from a mix of developmental, emotional, and physical or medical factors. Those more complex cases require a planned approach, which can mean including a psychologist, physician, and occupational therapist, as appropriate.

If the issue is developmental, trust the work of nature and maturation to do right by your child while you capably step in with routines, encouragement, and safekeeping in the interim. If the issue is emotional, you will want to consider deeply what is happening for your child that they need to use their elimination systems as a stronghold of control. Understand that it is your child's perception that is key here. Just as beauty is in the eye of the beholder, what is worthy of causing emotional upset is in the eye of your child. If your child has sensed that they need to step into the lead because of a perceived absence of safety in the world around them, that shift must be dealt with first. You are your child's big person. Even if you did not cause this perceived absence of safety, you are the only one in a position to take over. In doing so, you can give your child the gift of being able to depend on and lean into you for the emotional rest they need—not only to master the tricks of the toilet, but also to master life.

TOILET TRAINING IS a big and intimate rite of passage for little growing people and their parents. When it goes sideways it can feel like a glaring parenting fail. Always remember that nature has your back. Most toilet-training challenges can be resolved with routine, by keeping your energy full of swagger and devoid of problematic story, and by allowing development to do its job. Settle in and avoid rushing what is a natural process. Your child's body will get this sorted in time.

A Guide for Pooped-Out Parents

- Begin toilet training when your child demonstrates a natural curiosity for it, typically between ages two and three years.
- Routine and consistency will be key. Start with plopping your little on the toilet at regular intervals. Aim for about an hour between each and adjust from there.
- Never shame, scold, or consequence your child for toileting accidents. Similarly, don't offer rewards or copious praise for toileting success.
- Generously provide for your little by making sure you have changes of clothes and portable potties at the ready.
- Make toileting fun! Play some silly games or sing funny songs to let your child know that toileting is part of how we go and grow. Take the pressure off by keeping it light-hearted.
- Occasionally, big emotional upset can get in the way of toilet training. This is normal. Children express their distress through their bodies, and so upsets in their toileting routines can become the prime outlets for emotional dysregulation. Embrace routine and consistency while addressing the key underlying upsets and you will find your way through.

9

EXPRESSION OF
AGGRESSION

W HEN ONE OF my sons was two years old, I was presenting at a large out-of-town parenting event. I had brought my family with me, and the host community happened to have a children's fair taking place—the kind that has games and carnival food and an inflatable dump-truck slide. My boy spotted that slide from the entrance of the fair and could hardly contain himself as we stood in line waiting our turn. Finally, it was his turn, and he received a five-minute window during which he could go up and come down as many times as he could fit in.

As the end of his turn approached I gave him a few transition warnings. "Three more slides, love . . . two more slides, love . . . last slide . . ." When his time was up, I waited at the bottom to scoop him up, but he immediately tried to dodge me to climb up for another go. I was bigger and faster than him, though, so scoop him up I did! He arched his body back in a typical toddler meltdown and I held him tight. With a comforting voice, I soothed him with murmurs of understanding his upset and I kept his flailing hands from landing anything solid on my face. As I shifted him in my arms to hold onto him more steadily, he leaned over and closed his mouth on my arm in a hard bite. He managed to puncture my skin with his top and bottom teeth through a long-sleeved T-shirt. We got through it. Eventually I was able to settle and calm him, and we moved on to something else. The next night when I went to present to a large conference room packed with parents, my arm had a deep-red and purple bruise surrounded by my gorgeous little boy's teeth marks. Street cred.

The following day my son was ill, so I stayed with him in our hotel suite and nestled him on my hip as I walked the floor and sang songs to him. He was quiet and soft, in the dopey, sleepy state that sick children will often enter. He spotted the bite mark and reached out his hand. With a gentle touch, he moved his hand over top of the mark and said, "I bit you. You loved me." For real. My message of love was exactly what he needed to hear during that intense moment of his young life. He needed to hear from me that he was perfect, that the situation was overwhelming, and that I was his mama; essentially, "I've got this and we're good."

ONE OF THE most frequent questions I am asked is if parents should worry that their young child has become "violent." The simple answer is no, because their brains are not yet developed enough to be capable of violence. Violence involves an *intentional* use of force, a premeditative deduction to inflict some version of pain on another person. So, yes, though aggression can explode out of them, young children are never intentionally violent.

Developmentally, children younger than five or even seven years of age do not have the capacity to consider all the possible solutions and options available to them in any given situation (see pages 113–16). Instead, they will either try their best to change what is undesired or, when it doesn't or can't change, sob big tears or go on the attack. That attack is what gets called aggression, and it is born of a young brain that does not know how to regulate. The experience of dysregulation builds up in the brain, creating a stress response, and that agitation must come out somehow. The aggression that follows can be outwardly directed at another person or inwardly directed at the self, and it can be emotional or physical. When children are biting, scratching, head-banging, hitting, throwing, yelling, or name-calling, these are all displays of a young brain working out how to handle itself in that moment. And there is nothing pathological or problematic about that.

Unfortunately, our culture has infused the appearance of aggression with morality rather than understanding it more accurately through the science of child development. When a young child hits another child or an adult, they are characterized as behaving "badly." And when a child is gentle they are labelled as behaving "well." All of that is crazy talk. There is no morality in the growing of brains. The response a child receives when they are aggressive is what makes all the difference when it comes to growing their brain and infusing them with compassion. Expressions of aggression are evidence that your child is going through the processes necessary to their own growth.

Though it is important for adults to understand that aggression is a natural and normal part of healthy child development, this does not mean you just stand back and cheer it on. That would also be dysregulating for your child, and with mounting dysregulation, you might see more aggressive behaviour. Similarly, if you shut down your child because they have done something aggressive, you are also potentially contributing to an increase in your child's dysregulation and, again, this may lead to more aggression.

Instead, the child who is exploding with aggression needs a firm and loving response. The sort of response that makes them feel safely contained in the emotional embrace of a parent or other big person who will help them sort out their big feelings. A child wants you to see, hear, and understand them when they are experiencing big feelings. Children are meant to kick and hit, cry and have tantrums, throw things and scratch. Parents are meant to regulate the child with a caring emotional presence and a firm delineation of boundaries. You must take the reins of the situation and let your child know exactly what is going to happen.

For example, when a child is hitting you might say something like, "Gentle hands! We will not hit. I see you are having a tricky time. I am right here, my love. I will help you." Use a firm voice to tell them exactly what they will do, or won't do, and be full of love, calm, and compassion while doing it. They won't necessarily be able to immediately heed your directive, and this certainly won't prevent their hitting hands from striking out again in the future, but it will make them feel emotionally safe and understood. Your actions will increase regulation while simultaneously reducing aggression.

Now that it is clear why young children will fly to aggression, and that there is no need for concern, here are some key points to think about as you move alongside a child who may be struggling with aggression. Remember that aggression is how a young child's brain responds. They don't yet know how to be more grown-up in their responses, because they aren't yet grown! Your compassionate response and setting of firm boundaries will help them get there.

Focus on Connection First

Start by responding to any aggressive incident with connection. This is *not* a time to focus on behaviour but a time to focus on connection and relationship. This might sound like, "I really see how upset you are! Oh, my girl, I know! It is so frustrating! I am here. You are okay. We are good. We will get this sorted." The message you send with this response is, I SEE you, I HEAR you. Instead of rushing in to teach a stern lesson, be present to the truth of who your child is—a little human who is doing exactly what they need to grow.

Drop a Flag

Part of safely containing your child during an aggressive outburst is to let them know what must happen. This is where you drop a flag. Not deliver a lecture. Not teach a lesson. Just drop a flag. Flag drops are all about getting in and getting out, so the art of brevity is paramount. I recommend making flag-drop communications less than five words: "That must stop." "Gentle." "Hands are not for hitting." If you drone on about the lesson, your child will feel as if connection has been shut down; they sense you do not understand where they are. As soon as they catch a whiff of lack of understanding from you, the door to co-operation slams shut because that is how the attachment brain works.

This shuttering of co-operation is what Austrian psychoanalyst Otto Rank called "counterwill."[1] When connection is high, resistance will be low. And when connection is low, resistance will be high. You reduce connection when you fail to see and hear your child in their moment of struggle. They just want and need you to see that struggle and help them through it. The time for teaching the lesson is later, when everyone, including yourself, is calm. Only then, after you have created a sense of connection, can you enter in with some teaching and cultivating of good intentions for next time.

Invite Softness and Tears

When a young child has gone on an aggressive attack, the way to bring them back to a place where they can be calmed is to dance them to their tears. Yes, your job is to help your child cry. But this is a special kind of crying, one made of soft, sad tears rather than hot, angry tears. And the way you dance a child from big, aggressive anger to soft, sad crying is by being soft yourself. When you empathize with their big feelings as you contain their aggressive behaviour, your child will eventually soften, moving from explosive attack to surrendered sadness. Over time, the more practise your child gets with the loop of mad to sad, the better they will be at self-regulating and the more successful they will be at avoiding the aggressive behaviour altogether.

Around age five to seven years, a child will start to find their way through low-intensity kinds of challenges without meltdowns and outbursts. If you are growing an orchid child, this settling may take longer—even five years or more—as the orchid child has more intense feelings to cope with and must have a more mature brain before you see evidence of its prowess with self-regulation. With practice, this brain will eventually support the child with more adaptive energy rather than attacking energy. How do I know that will happen? Because that is nature's design, and when we support it rather than try to stamp it out, growth occurs.

The Sibling Battlefield

I will talk more about sibling relationships in chapter 10, but I mention it here because the sibling battlefield can be tricky. I am often asked how people can be expected to be so emotionally available to and connect with a small child who is behaving aggressively and has hurt siblings in the process. This is not a matter of choosing between responding to the child who is struggling with aggressive behaviours and the child who has been hit or bit or scratched. Rather, work on using multiple ways of connecting to the various children involved. You already have the tools you need: your eyes, voice, touch, and even your proximity. You can connect with your voice with one child as you come close to the other. Or keep your eyes on one child as you touch the other. As the capable big person, you do the dance to figure out which approach will be right for which child.

Check Your Own Response

When children act out aggressively, the response from the big person can be intense and fast and full of anger. You may even surprise yourself with how suddenly that can happen. You got smacked in the face or bitten on the leg and you might let a yell or a swat escape before realizing what is happening, and then you might be tempted to justify your actions. Central to your own growth and capacity to be in the lead for your child is taking the time to figure out where that response came from. In understanding your response, you may be able to shift your perspective, which will result in your ability to be more adept at responding with connection from the get-go.

As you consider this, there are likely two factors at play here—one is a neurological response and the other is the story you have chosen to feed yourself. The neurological response will be instantaneous. You get hit or hurt in some other way and cortisol flows into your body to ready you for flight or fight.

Dr. Jill Bolte Taylor is a Harvard educated neuroanatomist who spent eight years recovering from a devastating stroke and wrote about her experience in her bestselling book, *My Stroke of Insight*. Here is how she describes the instantaneous neurological response. She calls it the "90-second rule."

> When a person has a reaction to something in their environment, there's a 90-second chemical process that happens in the body; after that, any remaining emotional response is just the person choosing to stay in that emotional loop. Something happens in the external world and chemicals are flushed through your body which puts it on full alert. For those chemicals to totally flush out of the body it takes less than 90 seconds. This means that for 90 seconds you can watch the process happening, you can feel it happening, and then you can watch it go away. After that, if you

continue to feel fear, anger, and so on, you need to look at the thoughts that you're thinking that are re-stimulating the circuitry that is resulting in you having this physiological response over and over again.[2]

What does that mean if you're a parent with a child who's acted aggressively toward you or another person? It means that you need to flex your own regulatory muscle to stay present in the moment for that child for ninety seconds. One and a half minutes that could make all the difference for your little one. During that minute and a half, it is perfectly normal to feel the surge of anger rise up in you. You may need to bite your tongue and your cheeks and sit on your hands—whatever it takes so that you do and say nothing that will get in the way of your relationship with your child as you allow this chemical wave to pass through you. Think of it as having ninety seconds in which to find a way back to compassion for your child while you contain your instantaneous, biological response.

After that ninety seconds, if you continue to feel angry at or wronged by your child, you need to own that anger. Any kind of enduring anger you have with your child is story and not reality. Ditto with thinking of them as unkind, and so on. Continuing that storyline will only perpetuate your reactive response both in this moment and down the line. The biological response is over, so any action spurred by that response is now a choice. You choose your story, your reality.

As you think through what may have you sticking to your story about your so-called aggressive child, consider the roots of that story. Those roots will have nothing to do with your child but will be embedded in the story of your own childhood, or perhaps a childhood in your family ancestral line, a story in which boundaries were intruded upon. This could be a story in which you were physically aggressed upon. Were you spanked or hit with a belt or the infamous wooden spoon? Do you have a history that could explain your propensity for spinning your chemical response, via your story and thoughts, beyond the ninety seconds?

While you are thinking through the story behind your ongoing, spinning reaction to your child's perfectly normal aggressive behaviour, this is probably a good time to reflect on the experience of shame or embarrassment you may have in the face of your child's aggression. Do you feel like a failure because you have the child who is the biter or the hitter? Does a hot flush of shame creep up and colour your face when your child's aggression happens in public? Do you move to show all of the onlookers that you are a parent who is not going to let this kid get away with such terrible behaviour, and then find yourself doing and saying things that are decidedly not full of connection?

Anger is a projection of guilt. When you lash out at your child in response to their aggression, this comes from a place of you feeling guilt about your failure, your incapacity, your weakness. And yet nothing in life is random, which means that your lingering upset with your child's aggression, your imperfection in responding to your child's aggression, your sense of feeling overwhelmed in trying to figure out how to make it stop is all perfect. It is all happening exactly as it is meant to happen so that you can grow, and so that your child can grow. What freedom there is in embracing that! What if you could say to yourself after a not-so-graceful response to your hitting child that of course you were upset. You had that reaction but it is not the truth of who you are. It is not what you desired, and you will endeavour to fail better next time. This is what parenting is about.

No Apology Needed

Another common question that arises around littles who are acting aggressively is whether you should make them apologize and give them consequences for having hurt another child or adult. Somewhat related is whether you, as an adult, should apologize to your child if you have a yelly-shouty or worse moment in reaction to an aggressive behaviour.

In the first instance, young children are behaving exactly as they are meant to when aggression escapes out of their growing, still-immature-by-design, dysregulated little bodies. So what is it that they need to be sorry for? And why would we make them wrong for being normal? The young child does not need to apologize for anything, but this does not mean you let it all slide and do nothing. As the adult, you are meant to be in the lead. Your job is to contain the situation by providing firm guidance and empathy for your child. You should also offer containment to any other person who may have been hurt by your child, especially if that other person is a child: let that other child know that you are the big person, that you weren't watching closely enough, that you do not like that they have been hurt, and ensure they are okay and tended to as is appropriate.

Now, what if you react poorly to your child's aggressive behaviour and feel that you should be the one apologizing to your child? **Do not.** Adults never apologize to children.

To apologize to a child is to put them into a place of having to take care of you and release you from the burden of guilt or shame over your wrongdoing. To apologize to a child and seek their forgiveness is to make the child responsible for this being okay. Recall that it is the parent's job to be in the lead position (see chapter 4). Parents take care, provide, nurture, and tend. Children never ever do that for parents, at least not from a place of expectation. It topples the nurturing hierarchy of the parent-child (adult-child) relationship, and that is scary for kids.

Instead of apologizing, think of atoning. An example of what atonement would sound like is in the script I mapped out above, in the discussion of how to handle a situation where your child is aggressive toward another child. When you are in a situation with your own child in which you have behaved poorly, you might say something like, "Mommy/Daddy had some yelly-shouts today, and I don't love that I acted that way. That is not how I like to do things. And I want you to know we are okay. My yelly-shouts are all done. I have got this and I have got you, my love. All is well." And then you move on and endeavour to make good on your words. The next time you mess it up (and you will—welcome to the club!) you can do some more work on your programming and figure out once again how to fail better next time.

CHILDREN ARE GOING to kick and hit and throw—at least if they are having a typical childhood. Rather than getting wrapped up in a fight against aggression, focus on how the expression of aggression—with a capable caregiver close by to provide neurological and emotional support—allows for growth in a child's brain and their sense of self. Invest in the belief that all children can go big with their feelings at times. Children are big feelers with big hearts. What a marvellous thing! Instead of seeing your child's aggressive behaviour with your eyes, see it instead with your heart and with your wise, intuitive soul. Be curious about your own programming that might lead you to respond poorly to your child's aggressive behaviour, and find yourself growing alongside your child. Believe that your child's intensity, when it comes out as aggression or in any other form, will stand them in good stead as they take on life's journey. And take to heart that it is completely appropriate and natural for your child to bring to you—the big person who loves them more than anyone on the planet—their biggest, messiest feelings and behaviours because you are trusted to be understanding, compassionate, and empathetic. Know that you can see right through the aggressive reactions of your child as they struggle to respond and grow their brain while growing into their beautiful self.

Supporting Your Child through Aggression

If you find that your child is regularly flying to forms of aggression as a means of having their needs heard and responded to, here are the central ideas for you to focus on as you lovingly show them the way through.

- Focus on your relationship rather than their behaviour. Use language and tone that tells your child that you see his beautiful heart underneath the lashing out, and that you will show him the way. Your response should be fully informed by that connected energy.
- Use a quick flag drop to let your child know that the aggressive behaviour does need to stop. Step in with swagger in issuing this flag drop and keep it brief. Five words or less is your goal so that you can quickly get back to the energy of connection.
- Be big and firm and also be kind and full of compassion so that your child is able to trust you to handle all of their big feelings. When a child can trust this of you, they stay open to processing their feelings, which means those feelings can then be moved and resolved. The idea is that your soft heart will in turn soften your child's heart, moving them from hot, angry upset to soft, accepting sadness.
- If you are working to support a child who has some aggressive behaviours and there are other children involved, such as can happen with siblings, know that it is possible to respond with connection to more than one child at a time. You can use your voice or your eyes to connect to a hurt child while using touch to connect to the child who aggressed.
- Check yourself and your own reactions to aggression. Do you have a deeply rooted story that might be intensifying your child's need to behave in aggressive ways? Go inside and do your work.

- Do not require apologies from your child if they have acted out aggressively. Children are not to be made wrong for the natural occurrences of healthy development.
- Do let the child who has been aggressed upon know that you are the big person here, that you weren't watching closely enough, that you do not like that they have been hurt, and ensure they are tended to as is appropriate.
- Do not apologize to your child if you have responded to their aggression poorly. Adults should not place children in the lead position of being responsible for releasing the adult from feeling badly about a poor response. Focus instead on the concept of atonement, which involves acknowledging that the behaviour was not what was needed or hoped for, that it is done, and that there is a desire for a different behaviour next time.

10

SIBLINGS

BEST FRIENDS OR worst enemies?

I spend a lot of time in my office talking with parents about how to support the older siblings of new little babes, and how to manage developing so-called sibling rivalries. Often it is after things have become difficult that I end up hearing about it from my client families, although occasionally proactive parents trying to prevent sibling challenges will book consultation time before their new baby arrives. Either way, the topic of sibling relationships is of much interest to parents, and rightfully so. The addition of a new baby to a family is a massive change that demands adaptation. This addition also incorporates wake-up calls—those unsettling feelings or triggers that may flow through you and have you questioning yourself as you navigate this change. Initially, the introduction of a new sibling may stretch your parental resources, at least until you figure out your own reactions, and support adaptation in yourself and your older child. For these reasons, the addition of a new sibling to the family can be a big transition, and that can make for some stormy waters. But rest assured, calm waters are on the horizon.

As we discussed in chapter 5, your older child's capacity for adapting to this change will depend on age and development. Here are a few questions to ask yourself about your child's capacity to absorb change in the family:

- Is your child able to regulate their big feelings?
- Has your child started to see both sides of the coin, or are they still one-track Jacks in how they perceive a problem?
- What is your child's temperament? Are they a dandelion or an orchid?

How you answer these questions will determine the amount of upset and reactivity you can expect, and whether it will last for a short or long time. I once worked with a four-year-old girl whose dastardly little brother dared to invade her world when she was just shy of her third birthday. She was highly sensitive in every way. She struggled with sleep, hated most food, and had food and environmental allergies that often sent her to hospital with anaphylactic shock. To make matters worse, her mother had suffered some serious medical complications following the new baby's birth, which meant that this highly sensitive little lamb endured ten days away from her mama. At age four she was incredibly defiant, resistant to routine and directive, and waking three to four times a night. The sole focus of our "intervention" was to increase the "dose" of attachment and watch the child come to rest. She had mommy-child outings, special storytime with Mom at bed, little rituals through the day like special Mommy-daughter handshakes, goodbye cheers, and hello routines. It took four months, but eventually all was right in her world once again.

The Dynamics of Sibling Rivalry

Years ago, I came across a description that puts into clear-eyed perspective how the introduction of a new sibling might feel to an older child. Imagine that your partner puts an arm around you and says, "Honey, I love you so much, and you're so wonderful that I've decided to have another partner just like you." When the new partner finally arrives, you see that they are young and kind of cute. When the three of you are out together, people say hello to you politely, but they exclaim ecstatically over the newcomer. "Aren't you adorable! Hello, sweetheart! You are precious!" Then they turn to you and ask, "How do you like the new partner?"

Imagine next that the "new partner" starts wearing your favourite old sweater and your other clothes. Eventually, they want to use your computer to play games and they start sneaking into your bedroom to "borrow" your stuff. You get angry and tell them to stop. They cry and run off—and return with your partner's arm wrapped around them! Your partner proceeds to chide you for being selfish and suggests that you might find a way to share and be a little more kind. Yeah. That's about right. Rivalry has commenced.

New siblings are a big adjustment for an older child. Most parents assume that the challenges within sibling relationships develop because of an accumulation of difficult interactions between the siblings. However, the central reason why siblings don't get along has nothing to do with their interactions but with the relationship each one of your children perceives they have with you.[1] As in the case of the introduction of a new partner, the arrival of a sibling suddenly makes the child's most essential need— their connection with you—appear a scarce resource.

As soon as this perception of scarcity has occurred, your child will instinctively double down on their efforts to secure their connection with you. Usually this happens in ways that are loud and challenging. Behaviour is communication, so in the absence of sophisticated language, your child is likely to ramp up their behaviour to communicate their biggest complex feelings. Since your child knows intuitively that the connection with you is essential to their survival, you can expect that any perceived threat is going to be a big deal.

Not surprisingly, the behaviours around the arrival of a new sibling can be persistent and intense.

You may think you have done a masterful job of setting up your older child for sibling bliss, but if they pick up on your sense that you are about to become a scarce resource, then buckle up—the ride is about to get bumpy. It is almost impossible to entirely avoid some level of reactivity in an older sibling, but it isn't terrible that your older child will have some adjusting to do. As you will recall, no challenge, no growth. You don't want to erase life and its colourful array of experiences. When that happens, development stagnates and robs your child of opportunities to grow. But you also don't want to find your child drowning in too much challenge. The introduction of a new sibling and the ongoing cultivation of healthy relationships within the family must be handled with care.

The Relationship Shift

A big shift in any of our key relationships can create emotional rumblings inside of us. And those rumblings can leave us feeling out of sorts for reasons that seem beyond the grasp of awareness. Our most central need as human beings is to maintain our connections with other humans, so when the energy within those connections shifts in new directions, we can feel disoriented and unsettled.

Consider this in the context of the birth of a new baby. Your relationship with your parenting partner will shift. Where previously you would have had more time and energy to direct into that relationship, now you are caring for a newborn. Your relationship with your older child will shift. As you manage the feeding and diapering and sleeping (or not sleeping) of a newborn, games, trips to the park, and other routines that felt familiar and settling for you and your older child may taper off, and the relationship will experience a slowdown.

The shifts in these relationships (you and your partner; you and your child) are about a dynamic between two people. As your parenting partner or older child experiences the changes in the relationship, an iterative, relational loop is created. Their perception of the relationship has an impact on you and your perception of them, and vice versa. Round and round, back and forth. You worry that your older child is feeling left out. Your energy in how you interact with him is affected by this. Maybe you are a little too attentive or you let your house rules slide. Your child senses your unease and instinctively wonders what is wrong, which makes him feel unsettled. He starts acting out a bit more. You take this as confirmation that he is feeling left out. And the cycle begins!

Take a moment to consider this shifting dynamic in the context of your history. Your previous experiences, especially those during your formative, early years, are likely to creep back into your present-day life as you navigate this time of relational shifting. What kinds of shifts or losses did you experience as a child? Did you have a mother who disappeared behind the veil of postpartum depression when your new sibling arrived? Did you have a father who increased work hours to provide for his expanded family? Did you have an older sibling who always had it in for you? Were you an only child who felt lucky to not have to deal with a sibling and share the love of your parents? You likely already have an internal script for how this situation will play out. But if you have not worked through bringing that script into your conscious awareness, it is possible that you will replay the experiences of your past and they will colour your perception of the experiences of your present.

For example, through a process psychologists call "transference," you might reallocate your childhood experiences onto your older child. You may have an internal narrative about how upset your older child is feeling about the new baby, and that narrative could have this upset playing out in a more extreme way than need be. Now that you have believed your story, it will flavour your current experience and that of your child. In essence, you will have created the upset of a sibling rivalry with your mind, and it will then play out in your reality.

Perhaps you experienced a lack of provision from your own mother and/or father as a small child. They may not have been entirely neglectful by mainstream standards, but you nonetheless feel a loss and a longing for some connection that you perceive was not made available to you. Whenever you re-experience those same feelings of loss and longing through imagining them for your child, it takes you right back to being three years old, even though you have no awareness of this emotional age regression. You will then react and behave as a three-year-old.

Problematically, you may then take the transgressions of your mother or father and "project" them onto others around you. So now your older child—who has pulled away from you in the wake of the new baby's arrival, and has triggered these feelings of loss and longing in you—is viewed through your projection, or tinted lenses, as the neglectful persona of Mother or Father. You can assign blame and upset to another person when you perceive them through a projection. Indeed, when you view your child through an internal projection, this may make it impossible for you to see them at all. You may pull away from your child, which sets up challenge in your relationship. The child now perceives a loss in connection, and the groundwork for sibling rivalry has been laid.

To emerge out of projection and transference, it is important that a parent continually queries what is going on within them, below the surface. What are the programs that run you? And how might those be sneaking into your current-day reality and affecting the way you are *being* within your relationships, especially as a parent? When you bring these core beliefs up into your consciousness as a means of understanding how you tick, you can make significant inroads into changing the essence of how you parent and, in this case, how you make sense of and manage sibling rivalry.

Sharing the Load

In many families there is a necessary division of labour. Mom does certain routines and Dad does others. Grandma is good at one thing, and Grandpa at another. The nanny or caregiver is good at this, and the auntie or uncle good at that. Kids get used to how we be and who does what. These routines and your child's understanding of them make them feel safe, settled, and secure. So, when a new baby comes along and everything changes, at a time when they most need relationships and routines to remain stable, it isn't any wonder that the situation gets difficult.

With some preplanning, though, it doesn't need to be that way. Think through what the new way of life might look like once your next baby arrives. What will your time look like? What routines are you handling now for your child that you can start to gently move over to another member of your village, like your parenting partner, a grandparent, a caregiver, a friend, an aunt, an uncle. Begin by joining in a routine together with your village partner and your child, and then gradually back out of that routine. Eventually your older child will get used to having another person help with things like bath time, dinner, lunch, playing at the park, and going to school. The idea is not to give it all up. Instead, the goal is to share the load so you'll be able to rely on your village without your child feeling the sting of that change while in the throes of adjusting to life with a new baby.

If you are operating solo in this situation or if you do not have the help of a village to call upon regularly, think about some ways to have your older child sit alongside you. Work on creating routines that will free up your hands for baby care by gently supporting your older child to some increased levels of self-sufficiency. You can have a stash of snacks that your older child can reach and eat while sitting beside you as you nurse your baby. You can be the voice of the farmer in the story she is playing out with her toys while sitting on the floor in front of you. You can set up jackets and shoes at the door in spots that are easily reached by her little hands, and show her the toddler trick of how to put on her jacket using the coat-flip trick (YouTube this now, thank me later). You are not throwing in the towel and leaving your older child to manage everything by herself. You are simply finding subtle ways to smoothly meet your older child's needs while you are tending to baby.

A Heart for Every Child

Sometimes kids get the idea that the love of a parent is a finite entity, as if your heart can only feel and dish out a certain amount of love and no more. For a child, this is a catastrophic narrative. The introduction of a new sibling can have an older child believing the negative story that your love is a scarce resource. You can head this off by setting up your child with a more positive narrative. Children are not able to be introspective about their stories and the feelings these stories create. That is the role of the parent, and one you can handle.

The new and more accurate story is that parents grow a whole new heart with the arrival of every child, because each child is unique. Each sibling has their own heart inside their mom and/or dad, not just a special place in one heart. This is why a parent's love never runs out and is never used up by another sibling.

You can make this narrative more concrete for your older child by drawing pictures of you with a heart for each child. You can also present them with the gift of a little plush heart that you have filled up with love; they can hang on to that heart and use it to remember the special heart you grew just for them. And you can repeatedly tell them the story of the heart that lives inside of you for them, how well it knows them, how sensitive it is to the things they need, and how deeply it sees them. Tell these stories over and over, as a young child needs that repetition to hold on to the theme of this enduring connection.

Connection Takes Time

All relationships need tending in big and small ways in order to flourish. Look for and create micro moments that will have your child feel seen and heard: the sparkle in your eye, the tousle of their hair, the kiss on the forehead, the gentle stroke of a cheek. These are raindrop reminders that will fill up their special connection cups through the course of the day. Beyond these micro moments, think about creating some routines around a special time that you set aside for you and your older child to connect without distraction. This might be something you do together once a week, such as an outing to the park or the library. Or something you do once a day right before naptime, like reading a special book or singing a favourite song. Whatever the moment is, make it a time of genuine connection in which devices are turned off. The sacred purpose of this togetherness should be focused on the child and heart-centred.

The Art of Multi-Connecting

I am often asked by parents how they can make all their children feel cared for, especially in the more challenging moments when more than one child is upset or otherwise needs tending. Sometimes parents lament that there is no possible way to do connected parenting if you have more than one child.

But I believe that connection is not a prescriptive action. Rather, connection is a way of being. You can make this work in a single moment by being hands on with one child while reaching out to the other with your eyes. You can tend to your older child's ouchie while connecting with your younger one through your voice. You can give a precious item of yours—like a scarf or your favourite sweatshirt— to your older child to hang on to so you can be with her even while you settle the baby to sleep. The sky is the limit here, so think about how to connect creatively and know that your child will feel every wonderful bit.

Love Them to Tears

There is nothing more powerful than your child experiencing your acceptance of their feelings as you bring them into a space of adaptation. For your child to deeply experience that acceptance you need to fully empathize and validate their feelings. You collect their tears when things are difficult. You comfort and soothe. You verbalize understanding. "I know, sweetie. It is so hard to have to share Mommy," or "If I were you, my love, I think I might feel angry at our baby too," or "Of course you miss having Daddy to yourself—that is a really big change for my lovely little boy." Whatever soothing phrases of understanding you choose, your tone of voice and your presence ensure your child knows that you are picking up what he is putting down.

As you do this, expect the tears to come—you want to move your child from hot anger to soft sadness. Remember, the goal is not to fix the situation but to create space so that your child gets to grow. Through being available to understanding your child's upset and allowing them a wonderfully safe space to express it, you pave the way for keeping them soft rather than hardening. If they harden, they will bottle their feelings and continue to react more explosively. With softness and the safety of your understanding to cushion them, they can release their feelings and allow for the process of moving on that is part of adaptation.

Welcoming a new babe into your family is a wonderful event, though it's not without some challenges. But these are good challenges—the sort that will have you and your child growing alongside each other and separately, with an abundance of love to go around.

Sibling Rivalry: From Surviving to Thriving

Sibling dynamics are not something simply to be survived. With some foundational understanding these dynamics offer a prime opportunity to help your child thrive.

If you have welcomed another little love into your family and relations between your children have become tense, here are some practices and key points to keep in mind.

- Check your internal stories and extract them from your narrative about your children's relationships with each other.
- Plan for your new little's arrival by thinking through how you might share the load of childcare with relatives or a trusted member of your village.
- Make time for each child, whether in a micro moment of a hug or in a daily or weekly activity.
- Reinforce in each of your children the belief that your individual relationships are solid and there is more than enough love to go around.
- Practise multi-connecting. You can be hands on with your babe while you are reaching out with your eyes and voice to your other child.
- Focus on staying compassionate and understanding for your child so that their big anger shifts into soft tears.

11

THE TRANSITION
TO CAREGIVERS

T HE MOMENT HAS arrived: you are contemplating leaving your little one with a caregiver. This can be a particularly difficult time for children who don't understand why you have left, when you will come back, and if this new caregiver can be trusted! This transition is also often challenging for parents, who may experience separation anxiety of their own. At the very least, the thought of leaving your child with another caregiver has likely brought you to a place of contemplation about how to approach this experience of "separation." Whether this caregiver is a family member who has arrived to spell you off for an evening or an afternoon, an in-home nanny, a new daycare, or even a preschool, you will be the key facilitator for turning your child's face toward the experience of connection, even if the concrete reality is one of separation.

The Transition Begins with You

The place to begin, as with almost everything in parenting, is with you. Before you can be in the ideal headspace to navigate finding a new caregiver for your child, you will first have to navigate the issue yourself. Do you feel panicked or nervous? Do you find yourself seeking control, or feeling overwhelmed? Or do you feel indifferent, numb, checked out, offline? Or perhaps you have feelings of guilt about wanting a break already!

If you have a young baby, you might feel a particularly huge amount of pressure around this—born of your natural instincts and societal expectation around mothers being home with their wee babes. Certainly, one of the reasons that parental and maternity leave is such a hot topic is that science has irrefutably borne out the truth of how much children need their primary caregivers to develop healthy attachment relationships that live on over their lives in terms of physical and emotional health outcomes. This is why maternity and/or parental leaves lasting at least a year and preferably two years are the ideal in countries espousing contemporary policies rooted in the science of child development.

With all of that in mind you might feel enormous pressure, especially as a woman, to stay home with your baby. Although this may be the ideal circumstance for many mothers, it is not the only condition under which your baby can thrive. Successfully and capably introducing a new compassionate caregiver to your child's life can be a wonderful way of continuing to see your professional goals realized alongside cherishing the development of your growing babe. So whatever guilt you may be feeling in this area is something you must resolve as part of your own programming.

The emotions you are feeling about leaving your child will create an energy in the space between you—and that energy most certainly will affect the ease with which he is able to settle into the care of another. It's important, then, to take some time to process your "stuff" so that the energy you are emitting is full of confidence and certainty. You will do this by identifying your feelings about leaving your child with another caregiver and working to make sense of where those feelings come from. As you do this, recognize that what you are feeling now originated back in your childhood, and has been triggered into being by this impending separation.

Whatever your scenario, imagine that adult you is acting as caretaker to child you so that the big feelings still living within can be softened or even resolved. It is from this self-focused place of inner work that you are able to change the dynamic between you and your child when it comes to leaving him with a new caregiver. With your inner work well in hand, it is possible to effectively shift your focus to the true needs of your child.

Choosing a New Caregiver

Choosing a new caregiver for your child can feel like an overwhelming task, as this person will influence much of your child's growth and development. Here are some things to keep in mind as you begin to navigate this task.

- Start early. Many licensed childcare providers have waitlists of a year or more. If you know that you will be heading back to work within a year of your child's birth, get on those waitlists while you are pregnant. Be prepared to provide proof of pregnancy from your doctor before the childcare provider will accept your application.
- Know that parental intuition is key. No matter how glossy the facade or how fantastic the so-called program, listen to your parental gut. Never attempt to override instinct. Your gut is your soul speaking to you.
- Ask any prospective caregiver these two key questions: "How do you make sure that every little person you welcome through your door is assigned a key big person?" and "How do you assign key

big people to the little people you are caring for?" If they cannot offer you an answer that assures you they are responding to the unique needs of the children coming through their door, and especially if they do not have a clue as to why each little person needs a special big person, walk—no, run—right out the door and do not leave your little one in their care.

• Pick a caregiver who genuinely sees you as the expert on your child. If you slot yourself into a caregiving dynamic with another care provider who is constantly attempting to override your wishes in how you would like your child to be raised, you've got a problem. First of all, what is it within your own programming that has you opting in to this? And secondly, why would you surrender your own swagger and know-how to someone completely outside of your life, your family, and your child's existence? Step up. Step in. Take charge. The end.

With your parental swagger definitively in place around the choosing of another caregiver for your child, it is now time to shift your focus to how you will ensure that this new relationship blossoms beautifully.

Passing the Spark of Connection

The most important aspect of introducing a new caregiver to your child is to understand how the attachment relationship you have formed becomes the gateway through which all subsequent relationships must be formed. It is as though you take a spark from the connection you have with your child and, while holding your child's hand, reach out and ignite the light that this new caregiver will carry for your child. When your child sees that you are orchestrating the new connection via the connection you already have with the new person, he will instinctually be more able to rest into their care.

This means that when the new nanny shows up at your home to "get to know" everyone, or when you arrive at your child's new preschool for orientation day, or when you take your child to have a look around the new daycare, the focus is not so much on introducing your child to the new big person but on allowing your child to observe you in easy, familiar, positive interactions with this person. Your child might see this and naturally start to interact with the new caregiver, or it may take several more visits or interactions for this to occur. Either way, stay focused on ensuring your child just gets to experience this natural emergence into relationship via you.

Artful Introductions

Successful transitions to new caregivers often involve a play on the social psychological principles that tell us "birds of a feather flock together" and that there are "two peas in a pod." We tend to like those who like us, and to be more comfortable with people who are similar to us, at least in the early stages of relationship. As a parent, then, your mission is clear. Create artful narratives around a blossoming fondness between your child and their new caregiver by connecting the dots between them. Find something that is the same about them and capitalize on that as a way to highlight how much they belong together. Maybe they both love a certain cartoon character, a certain food, or a specific kind of music.

Making these connections might also sound something like, "Did you see the smile on Ms. Robinson's face this morning when she said hello to you? I think she is taking a shine to you!" And this works both ways! You might say to the caregiver, "Michael came home yesterday and all he could talk about was how much he likes the stories you tell him at school. I think he is really enjoying you!"

When my youngest son started preschool at age three, the school had a "meet the teacher" day about three months before his first day. I made sure to snap a few pictures of him with each of his two teachers. In those pictures, they both had smiling, warm faces; he, however, looked decidedly uncertain. I hung those photos on our fridge and talked about them often. "Look at the sparkle in Ms. Melissa's eyes in that picture. I think she was so happy to meet you." "Look at the smile on Ms. Sarah's face! It looks like she feels as though she is the luckiest teacher in the land to have gotten you in her class." When he finally started with school, I made sure to collect evidence from my son about his teachers, and then shared this with them in funny, short stories at drop-off or pick-up times. All of this connectivity will make your child feel more comfortable being left in the care of that person and will also nurture the caregiver's fondness for your child.

Gradual Entry

For some children, being left with another caregiver is a massive transition. If you think this is the case for your child, or if you have already had difficulty settling your child with a new caregiver, it might be a good idea to implement a gradual entry/transition protocol. Gradual entry allows your child to experience a literal transfer of the connection spark to the new caregiver. Start as you wish to go, which means that implementing a gradual entry/transition protocol after you have realized the situation is difficult is not as ideal as doing so right from the beginning. If you have a sensitive orchid child, or there are other things happening in life that might make the transition to a new caregiver a little more challenging, proactively implementing a gradual entry/transition plan is the ideal.

Sometimes there's no way of knowing how the transition to a new caregiver will play out. If all the signs were good, but the road is still proving to be a bit bumpy, a reactive gradual entry/transition plan is a much better option than blindly pressing on and hoping for the best. With a reactive plan, however, it may take your child a bit longer to settle.

A gradual entry/transition plan into a new preschool or daycare might look something like this:

- Parent and child come together, spend a short time (fifteen to thirty minutes) together in the classroom/daycare, and then leave together.
- Parent and child come together, spend ten to fifteen minutes together in the classroom/daycare, parent leaves, and child stays a short time (one hour) on their own before parent returns and they leave together.
- The child's time on their own is gradually extended to include one major transition at a time (e.g., circle time, snack time, lunch time, naptime, etc.), while the parent's time in the classroom/daycare at the start of the day is gradually reduced.

If you are leaving your child at home with a new caregiver, you can adjust the above accordingly, using the same general principles and themes. The speed with which each child progresses through this transition will be unique to their situation. However, a gradual entry protocol would be at least a full week if attending preschool/daycare every day, and longer if attending part-time; for some children it will take several weeks or even months. The important thing is that you take your cues from the child and adjust accordingly.

Coming Alongside to Get Them Onside

As much as you may have laid the foundation for an easier relationship between your child and his new caregiver, it is also important to facilitate the transition at each visit. A child needs time to switch from leaning into you to leaning into the new caregiver. Where brain development is concerned, this switch can be tricky. The key to easing your child into each transition with the new caregiver—both at the beginning of their relationship with this person and ongoing—is to ensure the new caregiver knows what it means to come alongside. Coming alongside is when the caregiver joins with the child in whatever capacity possible so the child feels some sense of connectedness. It involves having your child feel "seen and heard" by the new caregiver from the moment they walk through the door.

When one of my boys showed up at daycare, he would be greeted at the door by his special care provider (and yes, I asked if each child got assigned their own special big person!), who would exclaim over whatever superhero T-shirt he happened to be wearing that day. And let's be clear, Maxwell had an enviable superhero T-shirt collection. "Maxwell, are you wearing your Batman shirt today?" she would say with a big smile. He would smile from his face all the way to his heart and lean wholly into her care. Had he arrived, been greeted aloofly, and then sent off to find a toy while Mom made her way out, he would have blown around without having landed in the classroom and with his caregiver. His caregiver made sure he landed directly in her care by coming alongside to get him onside every single day, and he was like putty in her hands. He felt seen and heard, which made it easier for him to shift from leaning into me toward leaning into the caregiver.

Make It Predictable

When a child is facing separation from you, they will be on alert and may even become alarmed. Key to settling this alarm is to make separations as predictable as possible. What you want to avoid at all costs is having the goodbyes feel like a surprise, as this will have your child vigilantly on the lookout for the possibility of subsequent separations forevermore. The best way to avoid this is to script goodbyes for your child.

- Use a daily calendar so your child has a visual of which days are daycare or school days and which days are home days. Visual schedules—where the words are represented with pictures—can also be great for daily use since your child gets to track what is happening in their life generally. This works well for a child who is two to three years old.

- Use verbal prompts. If you are leaving your child with a sitter for the evening, you can use verbal prompts to indicate that this transition is coming up later in the day, and to highlight the order in which things will proceed. You could even use a visual schedule that shows "naptime ... then play at the park ... then babysitter." There are some great commercially available schedules designed for exactly this purpose.[1]

- Make sure you say goodbye when it is time to leave your child. So many parents fall prey to the belief that they can avoid the big tears if they quietly disappear, as if this is somehow better. In fact, it is disastrously worse. A well-handled goodbye does not mean a goodbye without tears. A well-handled goodbye means that the trusting relationship your child has with you and that relationship he is developing with his new caregiver are both preserved. When you sneak off, you give your child a reason to not trust you, and you create a situation in which he feels he must be vigilant in maintaining connection with you. Avoiding a goodbye creates a giant hole that will need to be painstakingly filled in and can make it difficult for your child to be left in the care of another.

- Create safety by developing routines around how you say goodbye. For example, a daycare "goodbye" routine could look like
this: backpacks and jackets are hung up, indoor shoes put on,
Daddy gives me a big hug, and Ms. Sarah takes my hand. Maybe
you have a little song you sing softly into your child's ear before
you hug and say goodbye. Whatever the ritual is, and regardless of the tears, make sure your child knows that goodbye is
happening rather than trying to sneak away, and then leave without fussing, knowing the replacement caregiver is capable and
trustworthy.

Create Hello in the Goodbye

The answer to supporting your child with goodbyes and separations comes in the form of creating more hello within the goodbye.
This happens when you redirect your child's emotional focus to
your enduring presence rather than leaving him focused on the
impending goodbye. For example, instead of your last word being
"goodbye," you might say instead, "I will see you after naptime and
when I pick you up we will go to the park." You move past goodbye
through to the next hello. A foster parent once told me a heart-
breaking story. One of her kids, who she eventually adopted, told
her years later that he used to freak out when left at supervised visits with his biological parents. Why? Because the foster parent said
"goodbye" and never "I'll see you later at pick up," or something
similar that would have allowed him to know she was planning to
return for him.

Creating more hello in the experience of separation can also
involve finding ways to be with your child even if you aren't physically present. You can leave something with your child that you
have designed to be especially significant for this purpose. I gave

one of my boys a plush-heart keychain that I told him was filled with my love and my kisses. It travelled with him to daycare and school, attached to his bag or his jacket, and if ever I was on a work trip, it sat right beside his bed.

You can also use rituals similar to those in the book *The Kissing Hand*, where your child has an endless supply of your magical kisses that won't ever wash off. Or you highlight the concept of enduring connection like that found in the story *The Invisible String*, which helps kids understand how we are always together. The parents of one little boy I knew who was struggling with separation took a photo of themselves snuggling him, laminated it, and attached it to a lanyard spritzed with Dad's cologne. That little boy wore that photo underneath his T-shirt every day to daycare. Once, when I went on a week-long work trip, I left my "voice" with my boys. I made each of them a recordable storybook, the sort where you record yourself reading and a sensor activates as they turn each page, allowing your voice to float out of the pages and into their ears and hearts.

The creative possibilities for generating a connective experience of hello for your child are limitless. But it is important that you consider the age and developmental stage of your child. Try to match your ideas with where your child is at from an attachment standpoint (see pages 65–67). Remember that babies less than a year of age are primarily attached through the senses, so things that smell like you, sound like you, and taste like you are important; as the most primal form of attachment, they also constitute the most foundational form of attachment. Everything builds on that.

You can also orchestrate the transition so that your new caregiver also supports a focus on hello. This person can script for your child, visually and/or with words, how Mommy will come back after naptime. If it is a daycare or preschool they can perhaps have a "family" wall that features pictures the children can look at and connect with.

If your child is learning a new song at daycare or making a picture at preschool, the caregiver can talk about how excited Mommy will be to hear the song or how happy Daddy will be to see this amazing picture. Your child will soak up every single one of of these drops of connection, and they will smooth the path of transition between caregiver and parent.

Caregiver Challenges

In Defense of Shyness

Oftentimes people talk about little ones being shy or "making strange," as though this is less than ideal. My perspective is that it's wonderful if a child is shy or makes strange when around others, especially adults who are relatively unfamiliar to them, because this means the child is following natural instinct. Shyness in children means that they are resisting the influence of those to whom they are not attached—and they are meant to. A child *should* have an instinct to pull back from other adults who are invading their space or are too direct. A child is born knowing that only their closest caregivers are meant to be trusted to be in the lead.

By about three to four months of age, babies have figured out through their developing attachment relationship that only these special big people should be trusted to adjust their world. This means that by the age of around three months you will need to carefully think through the separations you have from your child. Bottom line is that a child must never be forced out of their shyness; instead, he must be championed in his natural development out of shyness through the nurturing embrace of dependence within a safe and trusting relationship.

How significantly shyness is expressed by a child is more or less shaped by temperament. Feeling worried that you don't have a shy child? Don't be. You may simply have a child who is temperamentally like the easygoing dandelion child I described in chapter 5. In this circumstance, "shyness" might express as a child who quickly looks to you before accepting a hug from a somewhat unknown relative, or who is maybe slightly quieter than normal at a neighbourhood gathering or a new storytime group, even if this quickly fades into the usual expression of gregariousness.

If you have a child with a more intense, sensitive temperament, shyness might look like them avoiding eye contact or proximity to any other adult, hiding behind your leg, clinging to you when around new people, and so on. My own son used to do all of this, and would even go so far as to bare his teeth and growl if the adults around him weren't respectful of his space. All of this was a normal expression of his instinct to orient only to trusted caregivers so his needs could be met. Understood this way, shyness is perfect.

Tears Are Okay

A universal proximity-seeking behaviour of children the world over is crying. When our children cry, it is unsettling to us, driving us to stay close and take care of the tears. But this can sometimes become confusing when we find ourselves rushing to prevent those tears because we don't want them (or us!) to experience being unsettled. But the goal of "no tears" is not one you want to hang on to. Tears are a necessary part of adaptation and are key to nurturing resilience in your growing child. Your sign of "success" in settling your child into a new caregiver is not necessarily a tear-free goodbye. It is okay if your child cries when you leave *as long as* there is a nurturing, connected adult available to support him through those tears.

If any of the adults are uncomfortable with the goodbye and/or uncomfortable with your child's tears, it is up to them, as the big people who are in charge, to make sense of those feelings from a place of personal growth. It is not your child's responsibility to make the goodbye okay for you or the new caregiver. Along these lines, a child should never be coaxed into shutting down their tears, or to not "make Mommy sad," and so on. Allow them to cry oceans of tears if that is what it takes for them to come to a still space of adaptation. Stifling tears in the service of adult convenience or happiness never ends well for the child. Welcome those tears. They are beautiful and necessary, and never a bad thing, provided the connection is in hand with a capable care provider who can show the child the way through with nurturing support.

Challenging Behaviour after Separation

I remember coming home after work to my young children. Whether it was their caregiver or their dad who was home with them awaiting my arrival, it was almost a sure thing that as soon as I walked in the door my boys would go a little crazy. One would act out while the other would burst into tears or start whining loudly and persistently. Invariably, whoever was looking after them would raise their eyebrows with a puzzled look, as if to say, "I swear they weren't like this before you walked in the door!"

I may have been completely offended by their behaviour had I not understood how the attached brain works. Instead, I was thrilled about all of this crazy sudden-onset behaviour timed perfectly with my return home. Why? Because I knew it meant three things, all essential to the health and well-being of my boys. First, their behaviour meant they were in the "fog zone" of switching their attachment focus from whoever had been caring for them over to me. The young brain is not mature enough to be successful at sustaining attachment focus on more than one caregiver, especially during times of heightened awareness or stress. This transition back over to another attachment figure feels a bit disorienting to little ones, and so you may see this communicated in their behaviour.

Second, my boys' behaviour meant I was indeed one of their chosen comforters. Whatever stresses and angsts and upsets they had been holding onto were now safe to release. They would spill out in my presence because my boys knew with certainty that I would see them and hear them. I would make space for them. I would comfort them. What a wonderful, crazy welcome home!

The third and final thing this flare-up in behaviour upon my return meant was that my children had possibly gone into "defensive detachment." That is, I had "abandoned" them all day, and as they listened to the rules at preschool or daycare or from their nanny and stored up all of their little injustices and used up all of their reserves, their subconscious attachment brains held me responsible. Even though I had nothing to do directly with any of those experiences, I was to be faulted. I was the one, after all, who had left them in whatever circumstances they'd found themselves. Now that I had returned to care for them and tend to any lingering upsets, they would feel a mix of relief that would initially have them snuggle into my arms, and then, after an inexplicable moment of anger, subsequently shove me away and become stirred up about one thing or another. That is defensive detachment. First, your child is delighted to see you. Then he quickly defensively detaches from you in a subconscious move to avoid further wounding and to communicate upset. Once this upset is released, children typically move through this behaviour quickly to once again settle back into your comforting presence. Defensive detachment is a lovely thing; it means you are indeed your child's safe and chosen one.

So, if upon your return home, or when you show up at preschool or daycare, your child suddenly presents with an uptick in behaviour, never fear. The presentation of a range of behaviours—all indicative of dysregulation in your child's nervous system as a result of the transition back into your loving care—is not a symptom of something awful. Quite the contrary, these behaviours are evidence of a beautiful attachment relationship between you and your child. This is yet another example of a parent win—when a child saves up all of their most challenging behaviour especially for you.

How to Know When It's All Too Much

With some contemplative planning, transitioning to a new caregiver is more than manageable for the vast majority of children (and their parents!). However, there are times when it starts to feel like too much. Perhaps your child has spent months with a new caregiver, in a new preschool, or at a new daycare, and the challenge of settling still feels overwhelmingly insurmountable. If you have already used many of the strategies mentioned above, it might be time to consider whether or not you need to change course. As a rule of thumb, the following situations indicate that the child is struggling and requires deeper understanding on the part of his adults:

- When significant challenges with separation anxiety continue for longer than the first month of preschool;
- When you see significant behavioural repercussions at home, including persistent difficulties with transitions, larger, longer, and/or more frequent meltdowns than normal, and/or other significant changes in behaviour;
- When your child's sleep has become interrupted in a significant way;
- When your child cannot manage to be alone anywhere in your home, even when you are home;
- When your child develops physical health ailments that appear, after you have had them assessed by a medical professional, to be psychosomatic in nature (the mind-body connection)—such as headaches, stomachaches, frequent vomiting, ongoing low-grade virus, etc.

These are all signs that that it might be time for you to find some support as you work to support your child. Understand that this support is for you rather than your child, so that you can capably step in and find your way through. In selecting somebody for that role, make sure they have a strong understanding of child development and that they are prepared to work together with you—the expert on your child—leading the way. It may be that this work entails more diving into your own process of growth and development so that you can be optimally available to supporting your child through the transition. And it may be that this work will entail coming to a deeper understanding of what is happening for your child so that you can realign their world, and your efforts, accordingly.

TRANSITIONING YOUR CHILD into the care of someone new can be a huge thing—for both of you. Know that even if it feels difficult and overwhelming, that does not mean it is wrong. Transitions and change are one of the things we can count on as a constant in life. Your child will face this again and again, and in transitioning him to a new caregiver, you are giving him the chance to have a successful experience of figuring this out. With care and a focus on attachment, your child will grow into these new relationships, as will you, at his own rate and in a manner that champions his development.

Survival Guide to Caregiver Transition

- Identify your feelings about leaving your child with another caregiver and work to make sense of where those feelings come from.
- Pick a caregiver who genuinely sees you as the expert on your child.
- Remember that your attachment relationship with your child becomes the gateway through which all subsequent relationships must be formed.

- Nurture artful narratives around the blossoming fondness between your child and their new caregiver.
- Give it time! Gradual entry allows your child to experience a literal transfer of the connection spark to the new caregiver.
- Ensure the new caregiver knows what it means to come alongside; that is, that your child feels "seen and heard" the moment they walk through the door.
- Say goodbye when it is time to leave your child.
- Script your goodbyes so they are predictable to avoid the alarm in separation.
- Create more hello in the experience of separation by finding ways to be with your child even if you aren't physically present.
- It is okay if your child cries when you leave, *as long as* there is a nurturing, connected adult available to support them through those tears.
- Enlist support if your strategies don't appear to help your child adjust to the separation.

CONCLUSION
THE MAGIC OF GROWTH

ERE YOU ARE with a little person in your arms, ready to love and grow. You may be just getting started on your parenting journey and already you've heard people say, "It won't last forever," and "One day you will miss this," all while you have baby vomit encrusted on your shoulder and are so tired you could sleep standing up. Yes, there will be a day when your baby no longer instinctively reaches up their small hand to clasp yours, or snuggles down in your lap for a snooze or a story. Yes, you will miss that, but you will also love what is on the horizon. One of the greatest joys of parenthood is the sheer magic of witnessing growth in your child across their developmental span, so go ahead and roll your eyes a little at the tongue clickers who chide you to slow down and enjoy these moments when your child is small. Then find quiet moments of gratitude and revel in what is—right here, right now—and settle in to enjoy the stunning ride full of bright surprises.

Parenting right from the start means that as your child continues to grow, you won't need to untangle mistakes or retreat to make repairs. Instead, you will have set up your child to experience growth exactly as nature intended. Parenting well, with an emphasis on preserving connection between you and your child, does not create extra impediments or struggle. You will know that struggle naturally exists in great enough abundance, and that what your child most needs is empathetic support to find her way. If you have started off this way, well done. You have given your child and yourself a spectacular gift.

If, however, you are thinking, "Uh-oh, I've got some catching up to do," please know that this awareness and recognition is a curious gift in itself. For in the struggle to catch up you will glean hope, find solutions, and experience growth. As you consider this, take to heart that nature would never have designed a creature so delicate that some occasional missteps by a well-intentioned parent would ruin a child forever.

The amazing thing about neuroplasticity is that the brain changes and adapts to its external environment throughout its life. The brain also has a tendency to self-right, and this means it is never too late to give your child a good start. Never too late to get it right. Of course, there is the reality that the older the child, the longer and steeper the climb. The young brain is growing at such a stunning rate that there is incredible opportunity for effecting positive change in a relatively short period of time. An older brain is still growing and open to external influence, just not at the same rate. The older the child (or adult, as this applies equally to adults), the longer it will take for change and adaptation to settle in. The science of child development has irrefutably shown, via neuroplasticity and the tenacity of the human spirit, that there is always hope.

As you look down the road, here are a few actions to consider incorporating into your narrative of parenthood—actions I believe will keep you and your children connected and growing.

Accept the Peaks and Valleys

Development is not a straight line. The complexity of the different developmental domains (including social, cognitive, gross and fine motor, and language) makes development an intricate process in the early years—a constant ebb and flow, peaks and valleys. Almost by design, when a child's energy flows toward the development of a specific skill or ability, a commensurate drop-off in other skills and abilities may be seen. So, with a big language burst your child can suddenly become a little more clumsy than usual. Or with a big motor-skill burst, there might be less talking. Know that development is not going backwards but that there is a finite amount of developmental energy available to a child. As energy is harnessed for explosive growth in one area, it becomes unavailable to fuel continued growth or maintenance in another area. This will be much more noticeable in the young child (under age six) than in the older child; that is because the developmental domains are vastly more interconnected in the first six to eight years of life. Closer to adolescence, the brain begins a significant pruning process that occurs as part of neurological specialization and will eventually result in the child's developmental domains becoming more independent of one another. As this pruning takes place, the extreme swing of the peaks and valleys in the different developmental domains will gradually lessen. Until that occurs, the parental ride can be thrilling at times. But do not fret: the ups and downs are normal, desired, and exactly as they are supposed to be.

Slow Down

A few years ago, I was speaking in a community where I was invited to eat at a highly recommended local restaurant. It did not disappoint. The chef subscribed to the "slow food" movement, believing that food was meant to be prepared, cared for, tended to, and created with close attention to detail, time, and patience. To this day, that meal was perhaps one of the best I have ever eaten.

Now reread these words: *prepare, care, tend, create, attend, time, patience*. What if those words defined how we approached childhood? If we were to ascribe to a "slow childhood" movement, might the outcome be similarly spectacular in an otherworldly way? I think it would. However, the current culture around child-raising encourages parents to focus on the end goals. Children are meant to be "ready to learn" by the age of five. What does that mean? Aren't humans born ready to learn? Another cultural goal directs parents to make sure children are exposed to all sorts of extracurricular activities to make them ideal, well-rounded applicants for the school that they "should" attend. And the reason they should attend that school? Because it will set them off down the right path for academic, occupational, and life success. Really? Says who?

Move. Drive. Perform. Succeed. Now. Read that list of words and compare them to the "slow childhood" list. What a different feeling. What a different experience. Imagine asking a child to move, drive, perform, and succeed at the same time that their immature brain is growing explosively and they are trying to stay afloat in the process. This is a future-focused approach to parenting in which parents and children will lose their way. It is a scenario motivated by fear—fear that your child will be left behind, will fail, won't measure up. And by pandering to this approach, you may create the very situations you fear.

The superficially applied constraints of contemporary life and parenting are just that—superficial and constraints. We need to get out of the way and allow the natural splendour of child development to unfold. Children want to learn and are learning in every moment, in beautiful and applied ways that far exceed fabricated, direct teaching in a restricted environment. Developing a child's ability to learn isn't about plopping them down in a classroom at age two so they can be school-ready and successful. Blah! Sit back and let it happen. Give your child the experience of being immersed in a life full of connection, empathetic guidance, spicy variety, the great outdoors, quiet space, energetic play, and time—sweet, sweet time. I promise you the mind-blowing results will then take care of themselves.[1]

Celebrate Struggle

There is no growth in a smooth, easy ride. Childhood, and thus parenthood, is meant to be full of struggle. Your child is meant to have a tough go with things. There is supposed to be a tantrum in response to a "no." There are supposed to be tears when something doesn't go the way she wants it to. There is supposed to be upset when life changes unexpectedly with the arrival of a new sibling, a new school, a divorce. Incidentally, you as the parent are also meant to have a tough go at times.

A childhood, a life, with no growth, one that is sanitized and stagnant, is not what you want for your child or for yourself. Only when you walk in the dark can you truly know and experience the light. As Neale Donald Walsch so perfectly captured, "You could not know Warm without Cold, Up without Down, Fast without Slow. You could not know Left without Right, Here without There, Now without Then."[2] Parents, hear this. You want the struggle. The struggle is life and the birthplace of progress.

If you look closely at the trajectory of healthy development you will see that struggle always precedes growth. In chapter 5 I talked about how your child will have to rage and cry before she is able to cope with upset and disappointment in a more rational way—at least for a few years. Her brain will, with the passing of time and the amassing of experience, know what it is to be regulated and to consider alternative points of view. Your job along the way is not to fight the struggle but rather to celebrate it. Tantrums are a win. Tears are a win. Upset is a win. All of it is part of the pathway to full emergence and growth. Though it will test your patience, understand that all of this is a win for you too; like your child, you will find further growth and development.

Frustrated parents of unmotivated adolescents often ask me how to get their kid out the door, excited about life, learning, sports, and family—and appreciating all that they "should" be thankful for. Most of the time, this lack of motivation stems from a sanitized childhood, one where struggle was either squashed or erased because the child's big people couldn't tolerate it. The whining, crying, and screaming is deemed too much, and the child is ordered to "cut that out" or otherwise shut it down. The erasing of struggle is also born of an adult perception that struggle itself is too much for a child, and so the struggle or impediment is removed. But when struggle ceases, emergence and growth also cease. If your adolescent spent his formative years being shut down or deemed incapable, it is no wonder that he now appears to lack motivation.

Again, this doesn't mean you need to create struggle for your growing child. Life, with its normal ups and downs, will manifest plenty enough of that without your intervention. Instead, remain observant and empathetic, step in to shield when you know that this is what is needed, and stand aside to observe development in action at all other times. Make sure that your own program, your own triggers, and your own needs are not dictating your responses to your child's struggles. If they are, go inside yourself and do the work you need to do so that you can be fully available to supporting the amazing growth of your child.

Cherish Individuation

Individuation is the process by which your child gradually becomes themselves—a being separate from you in mind and body. The human infant arrives in the world completely unaware of their separateness. Sometime around her second birthday she will realize that she is an entirely separate being from you. Incidentally, this is also the time when you are likely to experience the full splendour of her celebrating this realization—a period often referred to as the Terrible Twos, but one that I believe should be championed as the Terrific Twos. And it is generally the time when there is a spike in the occurrence of separation anxiety. Realizing that you are your own person when all along you thought your mom and/or dad and you were one and the same is definitely cause for separation anxiety, especially in the orchid or sensitive child.

As your child develops, there will be other instances of individuation. Throughout middle childhood (ages six to twelve years), children move gradually from believing that they are you (rather than a separate being) to the idea that they are what is created by you. In this there is a little more room for your child to develop a sense of his emerging self. He will land on his likes and dislikes. He will have dreams and hopes all his own. He will begin developing his identity in earnest. With the onset of adolescence there is another big surge in individuation, when your child moves on to the belief that he is what is created by you and by himself. The journey through adolescence really becomes more and more about making room for his understanding of self as manifested by and for himself instead of defined by you. And just as your child experienced the sting of separation upon the early realization of his separateness from you, now you get to experience the sting of separation on this same realization. Know that the oft-touted frustrations of adolescence are simply your child becoming his own person. And isn't that what you have been working toward all along?

At this point you as a parent can be triggered into your own process. Do your own work around any triggers you happen upon along the way, for you do not want to miss out on what life is presenting to you for your own growth. And then rest easy. Nature is doing its job. Look at your child. Growing up. Becoming himself.

Discipline Mindfully

During your child's second year, you will probably begin to wonder what you are supposed to be doing when it comes to discipline. As a psychologist who has supported thousands of parents, it has been my experience that things can quickly get off-track in the world of discipline. Parents implement all sorts of tricks and strategies in the pursuit of good behaviour, often with the encouragement of popular cultural biases. This can include things like timeouts, consequences, removal of privileges, and reward systems.

However, there is a very serious problem with these tricks and strategies: they are a sacrificial play. They take your child's most foundational need—connection with you—and put it all on the line in the name of "good" behaviour. I wrote about this extensively in my book *Discipline Without Damage*. Good behaviour should not be used as a proxy for good development. Behaviour is just communication. So listen. Listen closely and respond wisely, always full of empathy and connection. Of course, be firm when that is part of responding wisely, but always make kindness more dominant in your response than firmness. As it turns out, discipline has little to do with finding your child behaving well, and more to do with finding yourself behaving well. Don't buy into the pursuit of good behaviour for the sake of good behaviour. Do buy into guiding your child along her developmental path with a whole lot of swagger and heart.

Ease into School Thoughtfully

For many children, their entry into the formal school system will be their first big foray away from the safe nest of home and you. Even for children who have been attending out-of-home daycare, there is nothing quite like navigating the experience of the formal school classroom full of expectations for performance and outcome. And your child needs to navigate this by himself, away from you (his one and only big person) and your restful provision of encouragement and nurturance. This transition to school life can create a significant experience of struggle for your child and perhaps for you as well. Most children will settle into the routine of the classroom, and the acting-out behaviours (such as defiance, more regular meltdowns, disrupted sleep, or heightened neediness) that kicked up at the start of the school year usually subside within a couple of months. The more sensitive child may take longer to transition; some children don't settle in until the end of the year or even until sometime the following year.

There are several things you can do to ease your child more gently into the school classroom. Talk with your child's educator about a gradual entry process whereby your child spends gradually longer periods of time in the classroom and away from you. Start by going to school together, doing a meet and greet with the teacher and other students, and leaving together. Then go together, leave your child for a short period, and pick them up for home time. Increase that short period to a longer period by gradually subsuming natural break points in the day. Your child stays until morning break, then start of lunch, then end of lunch, then afternoon break, and so on. You might also think of ways to "be with" your child at school, even when you cannot be there with them. Tuck a picture of you and your child into her backpack, fill her hands with magic kisses that never wash off, or place a special note in her lunch bag.

For other children, the transition to school can simply be too much challenge to absorb. It has them drowning in expectations, separation, and upset. No matter how you step in to soften the experience, the child may not be in a position to cope. It's much better to work with where the child is at rather than trying to hurry things along only to create a bigger problem that will need to be faced eventually. The solution here might be distance learning or homeschooling, or shortened school days and/or a shortened school week. If that is not possible, it's essential that the intensity of the expectations and felt separation be softened. Whatever solution you settle on, step in and do so fiercely. The long-term fallout from a push that came too early and too intensely is a far greater challenge to cope with than a delayed school start or a change in how "school" is delivered.

Cultivate Passion

As your child individuates and becomes his own person, part of your parental role will be to provide the sort of experiences that allow your child to discover who they are and how they roll. There are two key actions here. The first is . . . do nothing. Instead, create the experience of boredom for your child. In this fast-paced world where children are often hyper-scheduled and the pressure is on to perform, what your child truly needs is space and reprieve from that exhausting carousel of activity. In boredom, the world becomes quiet enough so that your child can hear their own voice, their own drive, their own hopes, their own passion. If you are constantly entertaining your child, you might be working just a little too hard. Sit with the discomfort of boredom—for your child and perhaps even for you—and see what happens. When your child says, "I'm bored," learn to say, "I love bored," and believe that you do. Magic happens where boredom is welcome. Perhaps with some initial pushback or discomfort, your child will soon have moments of really sitting in the truth of who he is, and as he plays and creates you will be in awe of the glimpses into this truth.

The second key action is to cherish a world full of variety. Sprinkle in new experiences and expose your child to many different things. Set about this intentionally. Even if your child is a soccer superstar, allow them to try out other sports, the arts, and other activities—while still making sure they have lots of down time and room for quiet and boredom. Even if your child loves cooking or crafting, set it up so they also get to try out other things. And as much as possible, rather than outsourcing this to others, step into the lead and be a part of these experiences. You be the one who shows them how to cook. You be the one who offers that super-helpful tip about shooting a three-pointer.

By including yourself in these experiences, you create a naturally occurring experience of your child getting to lean into your capable and knowing provision. Have your child continue to know your connection and closeness as you walk through the variety of life alongside them.

Give the Gift of Dependence

Contemporary child-raising culture is obsessed with independence. Parents are inculcated with sentiments like "You should not do for a child what they can and should do for themselves." The problem with this approach is deftly illustrated in the following two scenarios.

Scenario 1: Imagine you are leaving work for the day and have a million things to carry out to your car. You are tired and have had a long day. Your colleague is leaving at the same time, empty-handed, and lets you struggle to your car with your baggage.

Scenario 2: You and your child are walking into his school together. Your child has a gym bag, a backpack, and a lunch bag to carry. Your child is overwhelmed because the prospect of a school day is a lot for him to absorb. He asks you to carry his backpack. You let him know that he needs to sort out how to manage those things himself now that he is a big boy.

In the first scenario, most people would consider the colleague a little bit rude or even selfish for not offering a helping hand. And if the second scenario were presented completely independent of the first, most people would nod in agreement with the parent, knowing as they do how important independence is.

I call foul. I cannot make sense of how the two scenarios are different at all. And I am alarmed at the ease with which the second scenario is accepted. Unlike the grown-up adult who is left to fend for himself in the first scenario, the little human in the second scenario needs—by design—to *lean in* to the parent's safe provision. On the heels of my big endorsement of struggle, you might wonder at what may appear to be a sudden about-face. How did I go from saying "allow the struggle" to encouraging you to rush in and rescue? This is where the art of parenting comes into play. It is about the *being-ness* of the energy behind your response. If, as a result of your own angst-y energy, you are swooping in like the proverbial helicopter parent in a manner that trumps your child's emergence and evens out a perfectly traversable path, then stand down. If, however, you are wisely and intuitively sensing that your child is overwhelmed, or picking up cues that indicate the need for safekeeping, or even the desire for a bit of respite at the start of a long day, then step in. And do so swiftly, confidently, and without apology. No matter who judges or admonishes you for having cultivated dependence, step in because you know that this is exactly what your child needs.

It is from the gift of deep dependence that true independence emerges. Sure, if you force independence upon a child they might walk around with the facade of independence, perhaps appearing more capable for a time. But the sheen of this newfound capability will wear off. Right around the time that the child is meant to be bursting with emergent energy from somewhere deep inside himself, he will emerge with ... nothing. In the absence of opportunities for restful dependence, your child did not build up enough emergent energy to have it one day burst forth. But when you welcome dependence, when you cherish it and really cultivate it, there will come a time when you move in to support your child and the response will be magnificent. It might be the slamming down of a forceful foot and a loud declaration of their competence to handle this themselves. Or it might be the quieter appearance of a brilliant desire to "want to do it myself." Whatever it is, step back and nod knowingly, allowing them to spread their wings and truly fly, understanding that this is what true independence really looks like.

Fill Them Up

As your child continues her developmental path, understand that keeping her filled up is paramount. But filled up with what? With all things to do with you, of course—your love, your proximity, your care, your understanding, your empathy, your guidance. Child development is contingent on satiety when it comes to parental provision of connection and attachment. If your child does not receive her complete fill from you, she will be forced to look around and find other sources. At first, she might come flying back at you for more. If these calls go unheeded, she may turn up the volume to get more out of you, often by increasing the frequency and intensity of challenging behaviours. This can take the form of rudeness, defiance, or going after a sibling more often. I call all of this "attachment seek-ing" rather than "attention seeking." If that attachment seeking doesn't do the trick, kids will often begin to seek out their peers as providers. This can be disastrous. Kids are not meant to grow up other kids. Parents are meant to do this job. Do not push your child into the immature arms of her peers. You be her provider. Give her so much contact, closeness, and proximity that she couldn't possi-bly hold anymore, and then watch her launch into her own universe of possibilities.

You might have thought that this provision of you would be lim-ited to your baby's years as a wee one. While it is true that, physically speaking, your child will be much more independent quickly, able to dress and feed and toilet themselves, it will be a long time before you get to retire. As your child approaches adolescence do not be tricked into complacency. They may be walking around like a young adult, getting places on their own, figuring out their school sched-ules, and even driving, but they continue to have great need of you. Their brains will not be fully mature until sometime in their mid to late twenties, and science has shown that human brains grow much better when bathed in a continuous provision of connection. In fact, retirement from parenthood may never be an option!

Perfectly Imperfect

All of life is a story, every drop a made-up narrative, because life is experiential and not about the reality of what is happening. Instead, life is truly how you perceive it to be. Being a parent can feel challenging sometimes. Difficult things might play out for you or for your child, and you may feel fear and worry encroaching on your narrative. But what if you adopted the mantra "It is all perfect, exactly as it is"?

In supporting families, and indeed, in finding my own way as a mom, I have found that this lens allows parents to keep going, even when the going gets tough—sometimes horrendously so. But in finding our way forward, accept that reality will always be a surer path to peace than arguing with it. As Byron Katie says, "When I argue with reality I lose, but only 100% of the time."[3]

When your child is diagnosed with a learning disability or a serious health condition, know that this is their path and yours. You can either embrace the reality and grow within it, or rage against it and shrivel up from fear and anger. When you and your child's other parent divorce, and you see your child's pain in coming to terms with that, know too that this is perfect as is. Why? I don't know. But you can just know. Even if the whys are concretely elusive, you can rest in the peaceful acceptance of what is, knowing that from this place of surrender, your most remarkable action will be inspired. This concept of "surrendered action"[4] is a truly conscious place from which to parent.

Accepting the perfection of a beautifully messy and exquisite life, for you and for your child, is—and should be—your focus on this path of growth. This is your path. This is your child's path. How it came to be, how it will resolve or not, is not the space from which inspired action flows. See the perfection of what is.

You will find your way. You've got this. You go on with your fierce self. Parent right from the start.

ACKNOWLEDGEMENTS

THIS IS A book about growth and life. And its existence was brought about in significant ways by an eclectic group of souls who are themselves champions of growth and life. I am forever grateful to each and every one who contributed to its being. In particular, I would like to thank Maggie Langrick, president and publisher of LifeTree Media, whose unwavering belief in me and our synergistic potential together has been energizing. I can hardly believe the doors our partnership has opened for me to live out my best life. You are a rare find. I also have endless thanks for my editor, the amazing Sarah Brohman. I still am in awe of how you managed to find your way into my mind and its inner workings so quickly. Thank you for going the distance, for sharing your talent and intellect, and for believing in me and this project. To Jesmine Cham, LifeTree publishing coordinator: I so appreciate all that you do behind the scenes to keep things moving smoothly. To Setareh Ashrafologhalai, designer, for perfectly capturing the essence of this book. To Linda Pruessen, copy editor, for seeing this project through its final stages with finesse and precision. To Stephen Ullstrom, proofreader/indexer, for attention to detail and commitment down the homestretch. And to the rest of the team at LifeTree for all you do to champion the work of authors and, in so doing, change the lives of readers everywhere.

It is one thing to write a book and quite another thing altogether to find it in the hands of readers. To that end I am very thankful to ZG Communications for Canadian publicity support, and to Darcie Rowan for American publicity support. Thank you to both for getting the essence of this book and of me, and for finding ways to have the core message land in the hearts of readers everywhere so that we can truly change the conversation we are having about children. I am also forever grateful to my star assistant Tara Mihalech. Your superhuman ability to be all things and to keep the wheels of social media, press, and our online world turning is amazing. You are an absolute gift. Thank you as well to Lindsay Faber of Lindsay Faber Photography for translating my world into picture form as we worked to take this project to the masses. You are a wonderful artist with the most golden heart.

In my professional life I have been incredibly fortunate to be surrounded by amazing humans who have uplifted and championed me along the way. A special thank you to Dr. Kristy Goodwin, who in addition to having stunning shoes, is a wonderful human being and offered generous input and feedback during my writing. Another special thank you to Lisa Carleton, my sister and also an incredibly knowledgeable nurse and Board Certified Lactation Consultant who provided invaluable input to my writing. A huge thank you to my clinical colleagues at The Wishing Star. You are doing amazing things. You are change makers, and from my heart right to yours, thank you for what you do to make "our" kids' world go 'round. To Pamela Chatry, my friend and business advisor, I would not have become an author were it not for you. I will always be grateful to you for showing me how to manifest my own vision.

As a doctoral student I had the incredible experience of getting to learn alongside amazing people who have continued to show up in my life with wisdom and support. To the late Clyde Hertzman, who was so inspiring in how he really saw children. Your legacy is next level. To Dana Brynelsen and the BC Infant Development Program, the BC Supported Child Development Program, and the many other early intervention programs, agencies, and therapists I've been fortunate enough to work with. You helped shape the way I see and understand families, and that is no small thing. Thank you for everything you do to improve the lives of children (not to mention my life!).

I also want to extend a very special thank you to the parents and children I have had the incredible privilege of walking alongside. You are remarkable—each and every one. Your vulnerability, your commitment, and your incredible capacity for resilience is utterly breathtaking. Thank you for trusting me to be part of your journey, and for inspiring in me the message I take to all families: "You've got this."

They say it "takes a village," and as a mom to two beautiful humans, I can tell you it takes a couple of villages at least! Amongst these I am beyond thankful to my community village that steps in and steps up so often to walk my dogs, check on my cat, feed me, feed my children, drive to sports practices, drop off and pick up at school, and celebrate the small and big things in life—all of it with smiles and generosity. You are the very best. Especially the Osings and my girl Pilar. I am also incredibly grateful to my Circle village for seeing and hearing me as I walk on in my own path of growth. It is a wonderful thing to sit amidst your collective wisdom, and to know that this support endures. And to my extended family who love my children and care for each of us in your own fabulous ways. Included here always are Kateryna Holub and Fawn Ventura, who have loved my babies as their own and in this way are literally imbedded in the neurons and hearts of my boys. You are heaven sent.

Having come through a period of significant awakening and personal growth in recent years, I am also grateful beyond measure to some key individuals for their healing support so that I could show up and be my best self. Gila Golub, my gratitude to you knows no bounds and there really are no words. Because of you I know family. Because of you, I know love. Because of you, I know me. You are doing the most important work of all (www.GilaGolub.com), and that I happened to find you makes me one of the non-random (!) lucky ones. Thank you for your heart, for your soul, for you. To Yonah Dwor, thank you for sharing your gifts and abilities as a healer with me week in and week out. The depth of your work, your steady presence in delivery of all things, and the remarkable character that comes through you are divine. And to my beautiful soul sister, friend, and mentor, Maggie Dent. I will never forget the day you declared we would be friends. I can hardly believe my good fortune that the universe determined we would cross paths. Your mentorship, generosity, wisdom, and friendship have meant the world to me. My sister from another mister, thank you for believing in me.

And finally, thank you to my beautiful family.

To my mom and Raouf, and to my dad and Carol. Not every kid gets the sublime experience of just knowing that their parents have their back unequivocally, but I sure did. I am who I am because of you. I love that I am a brilliant blend of your stunning selves. I love that you were picked for me. With every breath in this amazing life I am living, I am grateful to you.

To my sisters Lisa, Christy, and Laurel. I have known tremendous love and support in each of your eyes. I love the way you are so spectacularly, uniquely yourselves and yet, we are also always "one." Thank you for being in my corner.

To Jonathan, my boys' father. This path we are walking hasn't always looked the way we thought it would. And yet, for every single step, I thank you. Thank you for being my greatest teacher. Thank you for our children. Thank you for our family.

To Nathan and Maxwell: I can hardly believe how amazing it is that you each chose me to be your mom. Nathan—oh your stunning mind and your stunning heart. Watching you grow as the incredible human you are has been beyond my wildest dreams. Maxwell—the depths of your compassion and the potential within you are staggering to witness. What a remarkable person you are. I love that you were entrusted to me. I am full of anticipation for all that life holds for each of you and in awe of all that it has already been. To you both, remember always that I love you more than all the grains of sand on every beach, more than all the stars in the night sky, and more than all the hairs on all the bears.

And to my love, David Loyst: I am grateful with all of my soul for you, for us, and for the life we are creating. Thank you for sharing your incredible brain, your beautiful heart, and your sacred self with me. You have listened, inspired, and supported me throughout this project in ways that exceed the bounds of this universe. Somebody once declared you the best catch in the Western Hemisphere. I declare you the best catch in the soulular universe. I love you. I love me. I love us. Infinity.

NOTES

Introduction

1. W. Faulkner, *Requiem for a Nun* (London: Chatto and Windus, 1919), 85.
2. H. Schucman, *A Course in Miracles: Combined Volume*, 3rd ed. (Mill Valley, CA: Foundation for Inner Peace, 2007), 11 (workbook for students).
3. Schucman, *A Course in Miracles*, 8.

Chapter 1

1. D.J. Siegel and M. Hartzell, *Parenting from the Inside Out: How a Deeper Self-Understanding Can Help You Raise Children Who Thrive* (New York: TarcherPerigee, 2013).
2. M. Wolynn, *It Didn't Start with You: How Inherited Family Trauma Shapes Who We Are and How to End the Cycle* (New York: Penguin Books, 2016).
3. See S. Tsabary, *The Conscious Parent: Transforming Ourselves, Empowering Our Children* (Vancouver: Namaste Publishing, 2010).
4. V.J. Felitti et al., "Relationship of Childhood Abuse and Household Dysfunction to Many of the Leading Causes of Death in Adults," *American Journal of Preventative Medicine* 14, no. 4 (May 1998): 245–58.
5. Felitti, "Relationship of Childhood Abuse."
6. Wolynn, *It Didn't Start with You.*
7. B.D. Perry and R. Pollard, "Homestasis, Stress, Trauma, and Adaption: A Neurodevelopmental View of Childhood Trauma," *Child and Adolescent Psychiatric Clinics of North America* 7 no. 1 (January 1998): 33–51.

8. M.D.S. Ainsworth and J. Bowlby, "An Ethological Approach to Personality Development," *American Psychologist* 46, no. 4 (April 1991), 331–41. See also J. Bowlby, *Attachment and Loss,* 3 vols. (New York: Basic Books, 1969–1980).

9. See, for example: L. Adamson and J. Frick, "The Still Face: A History of a Shared Experimental Paradigm," *Infancy* 4, no. 4 (October 2003): 451–73; B.D. Perry, "Bonding and Attachment in Maltreated Children," The ChildTrauma Academy, https://childtrauma.org/wp-content/uploads/2013/11/Bonding_13.pdf, accessed March 17, 2019; P.A. Fisher et al., "Effects of a Therapeutic Intervention for Foster Preschoolers on Diurnal Cortisol Activity, *Psychoneuroendocrinology* 32, nos. 8–10 (September to November 2007): 892–905; Siegel and Hartzell, *Parenting from the Inside Out,* 2013.

10. H.F. Harlow, "Love in Infant Monkeys," *Scientific American* 200 (June 1959): 68–74.

11. See, for example, J.B. Watson and R. Rayner, "Conditioned Emotional Reactions," *Journal of Experimental Psychology* 3 no. 1 (1920): 1–14.

12. J.B. Watson, *Psychological Care of the Infant* (New York: W.W. Norton & Company, 1928), 77.

13. "Five Numbers to Remember about Early Childhood Development," Center on the Developing Child, Harvard University, 2016, https://acestoohigh.com/2013/03/01/five-numbers-to-remembers-about-early-childhood-development.

14. See Neufeld Institute (https://neufeldinstitute.org/course/neufeld-intensive-iii-becoming-attached/) for details on the instructional course related to this study.

15. N.I. Eisenberger and M.D. Lieberman, "Why Rejection Hurts: A Common Neural Alarm System for Physical and Social Pain," *Trends in Cognitive Sciences* 8, no. 7 (July 2004): 294–300.

16. B. Lipton, *The Biology of Belief: Unleashing the Power of Consciousness* (London: Hay House, 2016), 176.

17. See the Raffi Foundation for Child Honouring (https://raffifoundation.org/about/) for information about the Covenant for Honouring Children, the related book with a foreword by the Dalai Lama, and the corresponding online course.

18. J. Hollis, *The Middle Passage: From Misery to Meaning in Midlife* (Toronto: Inner City Books, 1993), 9.

19. T. Hansen, "Parenthood and Marital Satisfaction: A Review of Folk Theories Versus Empirical Evidence," *Social Indicators Research* 108, no. 1 (August 2012): 29. See also J.M. Twenge, W.K Campbell, and C.A. Foster, "Parenthood and Marital Satisfaction," *Journal of Marriage and Family* 65,

no. 3 (August 2003): 574–83, and J. Glass, R.W. Simon, and M.A. Andersson, "Parenthood and Happiness: Effects of Work-Family Reconciliation Policies in 22 OECD Countries," *American Journal of Sociology* 122, no. 3 (November 2016): 886–29.

20. J. Campbell, *This Business of the Gods* (Caledon East, ON: Windrose Films, 1990), 78.

Chapter 2

1. R. Winston and R. Chicot, "The Importance of Early Bonding on the Long-term Mental Health and Resilience of Children," *London Journal of Primary Care* 8, no. 1 (2016): 12–14.

2. See, for example, C. Boecker, "Talk to Me, Play with Me, Carry Me," accessed March 12, 2019, https://vimeo.com/258695201.

3. See Neufeld Institute (https://neufeldinstitute.org/course/neufeld-intensive-iii-becoming-attached/) for details on the instructional course related to this study.

4. D. Casenhiser, S. Shanker, and J. Stieben, "Learning through Interaction in Children with Autism: Preliminary Data from a Social-Communication-Based Intervention," *Autism* 17, no. 2 (March 2013): 1–22.

5. D.W. Winnicott, *The Child, the Family, and the Outside World* (Middlesex, UK: Penguin, 1973), 173.

6. B. van der Kolk, *The Body Keeps the Score: Brain, Mind and Body in the Healing of Trauma* (New York: Penguin, 2015), 129.

7. J. Das, "Rabbi Hillel's Three Questions," August 20, 2013, https://www.speakingtree.in/blog/rabbi-hillels-three-questions. See also Hillel, "Pirqe Aboth, chapter 1," trans. Charles Taylor, accessed July 14, 2018, http://www.sacred-texts.com/jud/sjf/sjf03.htm.

8. K. Frantz, as cited numerous times in *Mothering* magazine, which she edited between 1980 and 2006.

Chapter 3

1. D.J. Siegel, "Toward an Interpersonal Neurobiology of the Developing Mind: Attachment Relationships, 'Mindsight,' and Neural Integration," *Infant Mental Health Journal* 22, nos. 1–2 (January/April 2001): 67–94, 86.

2. In *The Organization of Behavior* (New York: Wiley & Sons, 1949), D.O. Hebb formulated what's come to be known as Hebb's Law: "When an axon

of cell A is near enough to excite a cell B and repeatedly or persistently takes part in firing it, some growth process or metabolic change takes place in one or both cells such that A's efficiency, as one of the cells firing B, is increased" (page 62).

3. "Transcript of Hedy Schleifer's speech on April 20, 2010, at the TEDx-TelAviv Conference," Tikkun Learning Center, https://www.hedyyumi.com/wp-content/uploads/2012/02/TED-TALK-Transcript.pdf.

4. See Neufeld Institute (https://neufeldinstitute.org/course/neufeld-inten-sive-iii-becoming-attached/) for details on the instructional course related to this study.

5. See D.J. Siegel and T.P. Bryson, *The Whole-Brain Child: 12 Revolutionary Strategies to Nurture Your Child's Developing Mind* (New York: Bantam, 2012).

6. D.J. Siegel, *The Developing Mind: How Relationships and the Brain Interact to Shape Who We Are* (New York: Guildford Press, 2012), 14.

7. D.W. Winnicott, *The Child, the Family, and the Outside World* (Middlesex, UK: Penguin, 1993), 173.

8. Five Numbers to Remember about Early Childhood Development," Center on the Developing Child, Harvard University, 2016, https://acestoohigh.com/2013/03/01/five-numbers-to-remembers-about-early-childhood-development.

9. P.A. Fisher et al., "Effects of a Therapeutic Intervention for Foster Pre-schoolers on Diurnal Cortisol Activity," *Psychoneuroendocrinology* 32, nos. 8–10 (September–November 2007): 892–905.

Chapter 4

1. V. Lapointe, *Discipline Without Damage: How to Get Your Kids to Behave Without Messing Them Up* (Vancouver: LifeTree Media, 2016).

2. L. McLaren, "Don't Worry about What the 'Experts' Say: The Kids Are Going to Be All Right," *Globe and Mail*, June 5, 2017.

3. G. Neufeld and G. Maté. *Hold onto Your Kids: Why Parents Need to Matter More Than Peers* (New York: Random House, 2006).

4. J. Amundson, "Will in the Psychology of Otto Rank: A Transpersonal Per-spective," *Journal of Transpersonal Psychology* 13, no. 2 (1981): 113.

5. W.W. Dyer, *Staying on the Path* (Carlsbad, CA: Hay House, 2004), 144. See also Wayne Dyer's Facebook page, accessed August 31, 2015, https://www.facebook.com/drwaynedyer/posts/10151866740351030.

6. A. Douglas, *Happy Parents, Happy Kids* (Toronto: HarperCollins Canada, 2019).

Chapter 5

1. J.B. Watson, *Behaviorism* (New York: People's Institute Publishing Company, 1924), 104.
2. W.T. Boyce and B.J. Ellis, "Biological Sensitivity to Context: 1. An Evolutionary-Developmental Theory of the Origins and Functions of Stress Reactivity," *Development and Psychopathology* 17, no. 2 (June 2005): 271–301. See also W.T. Boyce, *The Orchid and the Dandelion: Why Some Children Struggle and How All Can Thrive* (New York: Alfred A. Knopf, 2019).
3. There are also lots of ideas about this in my book *Discipline Without Damage*.
4. B. Brown, *Daring Greatly: How the Courage to Be Vulnerable Transforms the Way We Live, Love, Parent, and Lead* (New York: Gotham Books, 2012), 73.
5. D.F. Narvaes, "Why Play with A Child?" *Psychology Today*, April 9, 2014.

Chapter 6

1. "Safe Sleep for Babies," Caring for Kids, accessed December 29, 2018, https://www.caringforkids.cps.ca/handouts/safe_sleep_for_babies.
2. See, for example: "Safe Sleep for Babies"; "American Academy of Pediatrics Announces New Safe Sleep Recommendations to Protect Against SIDS, Sleep-Related Infant Deaths," American Academy of Pediatrics, October 24, 2016, https://www.aap.org/en-us/about-the-aap/aap-press-room/pages/american-academy-of-pediatrics-announces-new-safe-sleep-recommendations-to-protect-against-sids.aspx; and "Controlled Crying," Australian Association for Infant Mental Health, November 2002; reviewed October 2013, https://www.aaimhi.org/key-issues/position-statements-and-guidelines/AAIMHI-Position-paper-1-Controlled-crying.pdf.
3. "Safe Sleep for Babies."
4. J.J. McKenna, *Sleeping With Your Baby: A Parent's Guide To Cosleeping* (Washington, DC: Platypus Press, 2007), 33–34.
5. McKenna, *Sleeping With Your Baby*, 34.
6. M. Weissbluth, *Healthy Sleep Habits, Happy Child* (New York: Ballentine Books, 1999).
7. M.R. Gunnar and P.A. Fisher, "Bringing Basic Research on Early Experience and Stress Neurobiology to Bear on Preventive Interventions for Neglected and Maltreated Children," *Developmental Psychopathology* 18, no. 3 (Summer 2006): 651–77.

8. W. Middlemiss et al., "Asynchrony of Mother-Infant Hypothalamic-Pituitary-Adrenal Axis Activity Following Extinction of Infant Crying Responses Induced during the Transition to Sleep," *Early Human Development* 88, no. 4 (April 2012): 227–32.

Chapter 7

1. R. Feldman et al., "Parental Oxytocin and Early Caregiving Jointly Shape Children's Oxytocin Response and Social Reciprocity," *Neuropsychopharmacology* 38, no. 7 (June 2013): 1154–62.
2. See, for example, First Step Nutrition (www.firststepnutrition.com); J. House, *The Parents' Guide to Baby-Led Weaning* (Toronto: Robert Rose, 2008); and T. Murkett and G. Rapley, *Baby-Led Weaning: The Essential Guide—How to Introduce Solid Foods and Help Your Baby to Grow Up a Happy and Confident Eater, Tenth Anniversary Edition*, (New York: The Experiment, 2019).
3. F.J. Elgar, W. Craig, and S.J. Trites, "Family Dinners, Communication, and Mental Health in Canadian Adolescents," *Journal of Adolescent Health* 52, no. 4 (April 2013): 433–38.

Chapter 8

1. T.R. Schum et al., "Sequential Acquisition of Toilet-Training Skills: A Descriptive Study of Gender and Age Differences in Normal Children," *Pediatrics* 109, no. 3 (March 2002).
2. B. Katie, *The Work of Byron Katie : An Introduction* (Ojai, CA: Byron Katie International, 2019), 40, https://thework.com/wp-content/uploads/2019/02/English_LB.pdf, 40.

Chapter 9

1. G. Neufeld, and G. Maté, *Hold onto Your Kids: Why Parents Need to Matter More Than Peers* (New York: Random House, 2006,) 74.
2. J. Bolte Taylor, "My Stroke of Insight," The Positive Encourager, accessed June 3, 2018, https://www.thepositiveencourager.global/jill-bolte-taylors-stroke-of-insight-video-2/.

Chapter 10

1. L. Markham, *Peaceful Parent, Happy Siblings: How to Stop the Fighting and Raise Friends* (New York: TarcherPerigee, 2015).

Chapter 11

1. Easy Daysies (www.easydaysies.com) is a great resource.

Conclusion

1. For some related inspiration see T. Hobson, *Teacher Tom's First Book* (Seattle: Peanut Butter Publishing, 2017).
2. N.D. Walsch, *The Little Soul and the Sun* (Charlottesville, VA: Hampton Roads Publishing, 1998).
3. B. Katie, *Loving What Is: Four Questions That Can Change Your Life* (New York: Three Rivers Press, 2003), 2.
4. E. Tolle, *The Power of Now* (Vancouver: Namaste Publishing, 1999), 208.

BIBLIOGRAPHY

Adamson, L., and J. Frick. "The Still Face: A History of a Shared Experimental Paradigm." *Infancy* 4, no. 4 (October 2003): 4451–73.

Ainsworth, M.D.S., and J. Bowlby. "An Ethological Approach to Personality Development." *American Psychologist* 46, no. 4 (April 1991): 331–41.

American Academy of Pediatrics. "American Academy of Pediatrics Announces New Safe Sleep Recommendations to Protect Against SIDS, Sleep-Related Infant Deaths." October 24, 2016. https://www.aap.org/en-us/about-the-aap/aap-press-room/pages/american-academy-of-pediatrics-announces-new-safe-sleep-recommendations-to-protect-against-sids.aspx.

Amundson, J. "Will in the Psychology of Otto Rank: A Transpersonal Perspective." *Journal of Transpersonal Psychology* 13, no. 2 (1981): 113–24.

Australian Association for Infant Mental Health. "Controlled Crying." November 2002; reviewed October 2013. https://www.aaimhi.org/key-issues/position-statements-and-guidelines/AAIMHI-Position-paper-1-controlled-crying.pdf.

Boecker, C. "Talk to Me, Play with Me, Carry Me." Vimeo.com. https://vimeo.com/258695201. Accessed March 12, 2019.

Bolte Taylor, J. "My Stroke of Insight." The Positive Encourager. https://www.thepositiveencourager.global/jill-bolte-taylors-stroke-of-insight-video-2/. Accessed June 3, 2018.

Bowlby, J. *Attachment and Loss*, Vols. 1–3. New York: Basic Books, 1969–80.

Boyce, W. T. *The Orchid and the Dandelion: Why Some Children Struggle and How All Can Thrive*. New York: Alfred A. Knopf, 2019.

Boyce, W.T., and B.J. Ellis. "Biological Sensitivity to Context: 1. An Evolutionary-Developmental Theory of the Origins and Functions of Stress Reactivity." *Development and Psychopathology* 17, no. 2 (Spring 2005): 271–301.

Bradshaw, J. *Homecoming: Reclaiming and Healing Your Inner Child.* New York: Bantam Books, 1992.

Brown, B. *Daring Greatly: How the Courage to Be Vulnerable Transforms the Way We Live, Love, Parent, and Lead.* New York: Gotham Books, 2012.

Campbell, J. *This Business of the Gods.* Caledon East, ON: Windrose Films, 1990.

Caring for Kids. "Safe Sleep for Babies." https://www.caringforkids.cps.ca/handouts/safe_sleep_for_babies. Accessed December 29, 2018.

Casenhiser, D., S. Shanker, and J. Stieben. "Learning through Interaction in Children with Autism: Preliminary Data from a Social-Communication-Based Intervention." *Autism* 17, no. 2 (March 2013): 1–22.

Cavoukian, R. *Child Honouring: How to Turn This World Around.* Salt Spring Island, BC: Homeland Press, 2010.

Center on the Developing Child, Harvard University. "Five Numbers to Remember about Early Childhood Development." 2016. https://acestoohigh.com/2013/03/01/five-numbers-to-remembers-about-early-childhood-development.

Chopra, D. *The Seven Spiritual Laws for Parents: Guiding Your Children to Success and Fulfillment.* New York: Harmony, 2006.

Das, J. "Rabbi Hillel's Three Questions." August 20, 2013. https://www.speakingtree.in/blog/rabbi-hillels-three-questions.

Dent, M. *Mothering Our Boys: A Guide for Mums of Sons.* Murwillumbah, AU: Pennington Publications, 2018.

Dent, M. *Nurturing Kids' Hearts and Souls: Building Emotional, Social and Spiritual Competency.* Murwillumbah, AU: Pennington Publications, 2010.

Douglas, A. *Happy Parent, Happy Kids.* Toronto: Harper Collins, 2019.

Dyer, W.W. Facebook. https://www.facebook.com/drwaynedyer/posts/10151866740351030. Accessed August 31, 2015.

Dyer, W.W. *Staying on the Path.* Carlsbad, CA: Hay House, 2004.

Eanes, R. *Positive Parenting: An Essential Guide.* New York: J.P. Tarcher, 2016.

Eisenberger, N.I., and M.D. Lieberman. "Why Rejection Hurts: A Common Neural Alarm System for Physical and Social Pain." *Trends in Cognitive Sciences* 8, no. 7 (July 2004): 294–300.

Elgar, F.J., W. Craig, and S.J. Trites. "Family Dinners, Communication, and Mental Health in Canadian Adolescents." *Journal of Adolescent Health* 52, no. 4 (April 2013): 433–38.

Faulkner, W. *Requiem for a Nun.* London: Chatto and Windus, 1919.

Feldman, R., I. Gordon, M. Influs, T. Gutbir, and R. Ebstein. "Parental Oxytocin and Early Caregiving Jointly Shape Children's Oxytocin Response and Social Reciprocity." *Neuropsychopharmacology* 38, no. 7 (June 2013): 1154–62.

Felitti, V.J., R.F. Anda, D. Nordenberg, D.F. Williamson, A.M. Spitz, V. Edwards, M.P. Koss, and J.S. Marks. "Relationship of Childhood Abuse and Household

Dysfunction to Many of the Leading Causes of Death in Adults." *American Journal of Preventative Medicine* 14, no. 4 (May 1998): 245–58.

First Step Nutrition. 2019. https://www.firststepnutrition.com.

Fisher, P.A., M. Stoolmiller, M.R. Gunnar, and B.O, Burraston. "Effects of a Therapeutic Intervention for Foster Preschoolers on Diurnal Cortisol Activity." *Psychoneuroendocrinology* 32, nos. 8–10 (September to November 2007): 892–905.

Glass, J., R.W. Simon, and M.A. Andersson. "Parenthood and Happiness: Effects of Work-Family Reconciliation Policies in 22 OECD Countries." *American Journal of Sociology* 122, no. 3 (November 2016): 886–29.

Goodwin, K. *Raising Your Child in a Digital World: Finding a Healthy Balance of Time Online Without Techno Tantrums and Conflict.* Sydney, AU: Finch Publishing, 2017.

Gunnar, M.R., and P.A. Fisher. "Bringing Basic Research on Early Experience and Stress Neurobiology to Bear on Preventive Interventions for Neglected and Maltreated Children," *Developmental Psychopathology* 18, no. 3 (Summer 2006): 651–77.

Hansen, T. "Parenthood and Marital Satisfaction: A Review of Folk Theories Versus Empirical Evidence." *Social Indicators Research* 108, no. 1 (August 2012): 1–36.

Harlow, H.F. "Love in Infant Monkeys." *Scientific American* 200 (June 1959): 68–74.

Hebb, D.O. *The Organization of Behavior.* New York: Wiley & Sons, 1949.

Hillel. "Pirqe Aboth, chapter 1." Trans. Charles Taylor. http://www.sacred-texts.com/jud/sjf/sjf03.htm. Accessed July 14, 2018.

Hobson, T. *Teacher Tom's First Book.* Seattle: Peanut Butter Publishing, 2017.

Hollis, J. *The Middle Passage: From Misery to Meaning in Midlife.* Toronto: Inner City Books, 1993.

House, J. *The Parents' Guide to Baby-Led Weaning.* Toronto: Robert Rose, 2008.

Katie, B. *Loving What Is: Four Questions That Can Change Your Life.* New York: Three Rivers Press, 2003.

Katie, B. *The Work of Byron Katie: An Introduction.* Ojai, CA: Byron Katie International, 2019. https://thework.com/wp-content/uploads/2019/02/English_LB.pdf.

Lapointe, V. *Discipline Without Damage: How to Get Your Kids to Behave Without Messing Them Up.* Vancouver: LifeTree Media, 2016.

Lipton, B. *The Biology of Belief: Unleashing the Power of Consciousness, Matter & Miracles.* London: Hay House, 2016.

Markham, L. *Peaceful Parent, Happy Kids: How to Stop Yelling and Start Connecting.* New York: Perigee Books, 2012.

Markham, L. *Peaceful Parent, Happy Siblings: How to Stop the Fighting and Raise Friends*. New York: TarcherPerigee, 2015.

McKenna, J.J. *Sleeping With Your Baby: A Parent's Guide To Cosleeping*. Washington, DC: Platypus Press, 2007.

McLaren, L. "Don't Worry about What the 'Experts' Say: The Kids Are Going to Be All Right." *Globe and Mail*, June 5, 2017.

McNamara, D. *Rest, Play, Grow: Making Sense of Preschoolers (or Anyone Who Acts Like One)*. Vancouver: Aona Management, 2016.

Middlemiss, W., D.A. Granger, W.A. Goldberg, and L. Nathans L. "Asynchrony of Mother-Infant Hypothalamic-Pituitary-Adrenal Axis Activity Following Extinction of Infant Crying Responses Induced during the Transition to Sleep." *Early Human Development* 88, no. 4 (April 2012): 227–32.

Murkett, T., and G. Rapley. *Baby-Led Weaning: The Essential Guide—How to Introduce Solid Foods and Help Your Baby to Grow Up a Happy and Confident Eater, Tenth Anniversary Edition*. New York: The Experiment, 2019.

Narvaes, D.F. "Why Play with A Child?" Psychology Today. April 9, 2014. https://neufeldinstitute.org/course/neufeld-intensive-iii-becoming-attached

Neufeld Institute. "Neufeld Intensive III: Becoming Attached." 2019.

Neufeld, G., and G. Maté. *Hold onto Your Kids: Why Parents Need to Matter More Than Peers*. New York: Random House, 2006.

Perry, B.D. "Bonding and Attachment in Maltreated Children," The ChildTrauma Academy. https://childtrauma.org/wp-content/uploads/2013/11/Bonding_13.pdf. Accessed March 17, 2019.

Perry, B.D., and R. Pollard. "Homestasis, Stress, Trauma, and Adaption: A Neurodevelopmental View of Childhood Trauma." *Child and Adolescent Psychiatric Clinics of North America* 7 no. 1 (January 1998): 33–51.

Raffi Foundation for Child Honouring. "Take the Course." 2019. https://raffifoundation.org/take-the-course/.

Ruis, D.M. *The Four Agreements: A Practical Guide to Personal Freedom*. San Rafael, CA: Amber-Allen Publishing, 1997.

Schucman, H. *A Course in Miracles: Combined Volume*, 3rd ed. Mill Valley, CA: Foundation for Inner Peace, 2007.

Schum, T.R., T.M. Kolb, T.L. McAuliffe, M.D. Simms, R.L. Underhill, and M. Lewis. "Sequential Acquisition of Toilet-Training Skills: A Descriptive Study of Gender and Age Differences in Normal Children." *Pediatrics* 109, no. 3 (March 2002): E48.

Siegel, D.J. *The Developing Mind: How Relationships and the Brain Interact to Shape Who We Are*, 2nd ed. New York: Guildford Press, 2012.

Siegel, D.J. "Toward an Interpersonal Neurobiology of the Developing Mind: Attachment Relationships, 'Mindsight,' and Neural Integration." *Infant Mental Health Journal* 22, nos. 1–2 (January/April 2001): 67–94.

Siegel, D.J., and T.P. Bryson. *The Whole-Brain Child: 12 Revolutionary Strategies to Nurture Your Child's Developing Mind*. New York: Bantam, 2012.

Siegel, D.J., and M. Hartzell. *Parenting from the Inside Out: How a Deeper Self-Understanding Can Help You Raise Children Who Thrive*. New York: TarcherPerigree, 2013.

Tikkun Learning Center. "Transcript of Hedy Schleifer's speech on April 20, 2010, at the TEDxTelAviv Conference." https://www.hedyyumi.com/wp-content/uploads/2012/02/TED-TALK-Transcript.pdf. Accessed February 12, 2019.

Tolle, E. *The Power of Now: A Guide to Spiritual Enlightenment*. Vancouver: Namaste Publishing, 2004.

Tsabary, S. *The Conscious Parent: Transforming Ourselves, Empowering Our Children*. Vancouver, BC: Namaste Publishing, 2010.

Twenge, J.M., W.K. Campbell, and C.A. Foster. "Parenthood and Marital Satisfaction." *Journal of Marriage and Family* 65, no. 3 (August 2003): 574–83.

Van der Kolk, B. *The Body Keeps the Score: Brain, Mind and Body in the Healing of Trauma*. New York: Penguin, 2015.

Walsch, N.D. *The Little Soul and the Sun* (Charlottesville, VA: Hampton Roads Publishing, 1998).

Watson, J.B. *Behaviorism*. New York: People's Institute Publishing Company, 1924.

Watson, J.B. *Psychological Care of the Infant*. New York: W.W. Norton & Company, 1926.

Watson, J.B., and R. Rayner. "Conditioned Emotional Reactions." *Journal of Experimental Psychology* 3 no. 1 (1920): 1–14.

Weissbluth, M. *Healthy Sleep Habits, Happy Child*. New York: Ballentine Books, 1999.

Winnicott, D.W. *The Child, the Family, and the Outside World*. Middlesex, UK: Penguin, 1973.

Winston, R., and R. Chicot. "The Importance of Early Bonding on the Long-term Mental Health and Resilience of Children." *London Journal of Primary Care* 8, no. 1 (2016): 12–14.

Wolynn, M. *It Didn't Start with You: How Inherited Family Trauma Shapes Who We Are and How to End the Cycle*. New York: Penguin Books, 2016.

INDEX

D R. VANESSA LAPOINTE is the author of the bestselling *Discipline Without Damage*. She is also the founder of The Wishing Star Lapointe Developmental Clinic. She has supported families and children for more than fifteen years and is a sought-after lecturer. She lives in Vancouver, Canada, with her partner and two sons.

drvanessalapointe.com
@dr.vanessalapointe
Dr Vanessa Lapointe

www.ingramcontent.com/pod-product-compliance
Lightning Source LLC
Chambersburg PA
CBHW021713120626
46545CB00004B/1546